# Computer Visualization

## An Integrated Approach
## for Interior Design and Architecture

**Wei Dong**
**with Kathleen Gibson**

**McGraw-Hill**

Washington, D.C.  Auckland  Bogotá
London  Madrid  Mexico City  Milan
New Delhi  San Juan  Singapore
Sydney  Tokyo  Toronto

**Library of Congress Cataloging-in-Publication Data**

Dong, Wei.
    Computer visualization : an integrated approach for interior
design and architecture / Wei Dong, Kathleen Gibson.
       p.    cm.
    Includes bibliographical references and index.
    ISBN 0-07-018012-1
    1. Architecture—Data processing.  2. Interior decoration—Data
processing.  3. Visualization.  4. Computer graphics.  5. Image
processing—Digital techniques.  I. Gibson, Kathleen (Kathleen J.)
II. Title.
NA2728.D66   1998
746.44'20433'0942—dc21
                                    98-48510
                                       CIP

*McGraw-Hill*

*A Division of The **McGraw·Hill** Companies*

1 2 3 4 5 6 7 8 9 0  1IMP/1IMP  9 0 3 2 1 0 9 8

P/N 018136-5
Part of
ISBN 0-07-018012-1

*The sponsoring editor for this book was Wendy Lochner, the editing
supervisor was Caroline R. Levine, the designer was Sara Teasdale,
and the production supervisor was Sherri Souffrance.*

*Printed and bound by Print Vison.*

# Table of Contents

# Acknowledgements

Years of searching for appropriate texts with no success became the impetus for this book — a book written specifically for students of interior and architectural design. Inspiration and ideas for this book have come from a multitude of individuals and as many experiences. Most notable are the design students we teach, who, through interaction in our classroom, have enabled us to become better educators. A very special thanks is given:

To Wendy Lochner, McGraw-Hill senior editor, a special thank you for your confidence in us to finish the book. Wendy's encouragement, professional support, and advice, as well as her good management, provided a productive environment in which we could accomplish this task.

To Sue Reindollar, Ph.D., our editor, and Carol Levine, our editor at McGraw-Hill, who helped to organize and focus the writings of two authors into a unified manuscript.

To Mr. Daniel Schoenfeld, who has contributed a great deal of technical information to Chapters 2, 6, 7 and 8. Mr. Schoenfeld's technical knowledge has not only enriched several applications in the book, but it has also helped to make the more technical content easier to read.

In the summer of 1995, the Graduate School and the School of Human Ecology at the University of Wisconsin-Madison funded Professor Wei Dong's research project, entitled *Visualizing the Built Environment Under Special Conditions: Visual Series and Guidelines.* This funding enabled Ms. Veronica Schroeder to become our research project assistant. She put great effort into this project and her assistance helped to form some of the framework for several chapters in the book.

The quality of the graphic layout and format of the book reflect Sara Teasdale's high standard of professionalism.

And to our students and colleagues who have contributed generously to this book in ways tangible and intangible: Christopher Budd, Terry Boyd, Praima Chayutsahakij, Brian Davies, Flad & Associates, Mindy Graves, Michael Hunt, Jan Jennings, Steven Laput, Teresa Martin, Janetta McCoy, Meanne Mercer, Wendy O'Neill, Eunmi Park, Ed Pope, Rita Serpe, Nicole Sharp, Diane Sheehan, James Sipes, Strang, Inc., Ann Wang, Susan Wong, and Bancha Wongkittwimol.

# Preface

Hundreds of books and videos about computer graphics are currently housed on bookshelves around the world. You may be wondering what makes *Computer Visualization: An Integrated Approach for Interior Design and Architecture* stand apart from all the others? First, the authors created and organized the book according to design topics instead of software topics. Second, the book uses tutorials and case studies pertinent to individuals interested in the creative fields of interior design and architecture. Finally, this book does not focus exclusively on one software but demonstrates the strengths and limitations of five different types of commercially available graphics packages. These three unique characteristics make this text different from any book currently available.

## Software and Exercises

Five software packages were chosen for this book because of their wide use in the interior design and architecture professions. Although most people are probably familiar with AutoCAD for two-dimensional (2D) drafting capabilities, this book will focus entirely on the three-dimensional (3D) features of **AutoCAD**. Exercises will enable the reader to construct solid models of interior objects and environments. **3D Studio R4** is a sophisticated 3D modeling, digital rendering, and animation program. This software package has been used in five chapters for various exercises. Readers will learn how to create realistic materials and apply them to wireframe models; lighting and shadow casting will be explored to add drama to an interior scene; and finally an interior walk-through will be produced using 3D Studio. **3D Studio MAX** is a new version of 3D Studio with a totally new graphics interface and many advanced features in modeling, rendering, and animation. **Animator Pro** is a 2D paint and animation software that enables you to create dynamic presentations on a personal computer. **Adobe Photoshop** is a powerful imaging and 2D painting program. Photoshop exercises include color manipulation for surface design and scanning images for portfolio presentation. For alternative graphics applications, additional sources are noted in Software Resources.

## Book Topics and Organization

Unlike most tutorial-based texts, this book is created and organized according to specific content areas within the discipline of interior design and architecture. Topics range from basic color theory to model building, materials, lighting, and animation. This method of creation and organization was selected to allow the reader to progress at his or her own pace, choosing topics in a nonsequential manner to match individual interests. For education programs, individual chapters may be easily introduced into existing design courses when a separate computer graphics course is not feasible. Likewise, practitioners can select individual chapters to introduce as appropriate projects become available.

The approach is practical and straightforward. An important part of understanding and applying computer graphics is providing a direct link with current design processes and contexts. Without this knowledge, computer graphics is easily viewed by many as child's play. However, drawing a strong connection to design principles and theories provides greater awareness of the computer's potential in design and its ability to aid in visual communication.

Chapters contain three key components: concepts, cognition, and applications. Concepts provide a theoretical background of design and computing principles, cognition focuses on subject definitions and methods, and applications concentrates on unique examples and case studies which challenge the standard perception of computer-aided design (CAD). This structure is intended to expand the reader's understanding of electronic media and its use throughout the design process.

### Requirements

Readers should have a basic understanding of how the computer works and some familiarity with DOS and Windows. Installation of software is the responsibility of the reader and will not be covered in this book.

### Conventions Used in This Book

**Bold** indicates the first appearance of a new term; for example, **Value** refers to the lightness or darkness of a color.

A capitalized noun indicates the name of a menu, panel, or palette in a software, such as "...in the Tools panel click on **Pen**."

**Bold italic** indicates the action of clicking a button or activating a submenu; it is also used for entering text.

**BOLD** is used for all filenames contained on the attached CD-ROM; for example, "open **TABLE.TIF**."

CAPITALS are used for both pull-down menus and stationary menus which are always present on the screen.

*Italic* is used for all buttons and to indicate when readers must input something, such as typing a name for a layer.

\*\*\*\\\*\*\*\\\*\*\* represents the order in which menus should be opened. For example, in **LIGHT\\*Omni*\\*Create*** the first word indicates a pull-down or stationary menu and the following two words indicate submenus.

[\*\*\*] represents operations which are to be done using the keyboard.

## CD-ROM and Plug-in Information

The files on the attached CD are to be used to complete the Applications sections in the book only. In each chapter certain files need specific software to open. Specifically, .dwg files need AutoCad; .3ds files need 3D Studio R4; .max files need 3D Studio MAX or 3D Studio VIZ; .flic files need 3D Studio R4 or Animator Pro; .tif, .jpg, and .gif files need Photoshop; and .avi files need Indeo Codec 3 or higher (This compression scheme is available free from Intel at http://developer.intel.com/ial/indeo/video/driver.htm).

Before any tutorial that involves 3D Studio MAX is begun, it is important to note that although all the procedures can be accomplished using the standard set of Max plug-ins, several additional plug-ins were used to create the tutorials. These plug-ins can be downloaded from the Internet, at Kinetix's hame site (www.ktx.com). Some of the plug-ins may come in an executable format (*.exe); if this is the case, simply double-click the file and follow the on-screen instructions. All other plug-ins will be in a compressed format (*.zip). To install these plug-ins, do the following: First, use a decompression utility such as Winzip (also available on the Internet) to unzip or decompress the file. Second, copy any file with the extension .hlp, .cnt, .txt, or .wri to the 3DMAX\HELP directory. Although not every plug-in will have a help file, if one is present make sure to read it for any additional instructions it may contain. Third, copy all remaining files to the 3DMAX\PLUG-INS directory. All these tutorials have been written using 3D Studio MAX version 1.2. If you do not have version

1.2, it is available free of charge from Kinetix. If you need to obtain a copy of the updated version, please visit Kinetix's web site at the URL listed above for more information.

If you should choose, for any reason, not to get the plug-ins or update your version of MAX, the sample files included with the tutorials will cause Max to display an error message stating that several plug-ins are missing. You may still open the files by clicking **OK** to dismiss the error message. When the files are opened in this fashion, however, several items (i.e., combustion apparatus, etc.) will be missing, and the file will not render accurately. Furthermore, before you open the sample files, make sure to copy all the files in the "MAPS" directory of each tutorial folder on the included CD-ROM to the 3DMAX\MAPS directory on your computer. This will ensure that all the maps and materials used in the sample files are present when you open the files.

## List of alternate Plug-ins:

| Plug-in Name | File-name | Author |
|---|---|---|
| 1. Blur fire | BlurPak2 | Blur Studios |
| 2. Particle+\blend | Part | Peter Watje |
| 3. TorusKnot | Knot | Scott Morrison |
| 4. FFDMOD | FFDMOD | Yost Group, Inc. |

## Resources

The best way to learn about computer visualization is to use the software. Unfortunately, it is impossible to teach the concept and techniques for computer visualization without choosing a specific software package to use. Again, in this book, the explanation of all the application concepts and processes can be shared by using most other softwares, such as Lightscape, Softimage 3D, MiniCad, CoreCAD, TriSpactives, TrueSpace2, Infiniti-D, CorelDRAW, and many others. We have collected a list of some examples of CAD software in the **Software Resource** section for you to use as a software reference.

# THE EVOLUTION AND INTEGRATION OF DIGITAL GRAPHICS

1

**Because the computer was devoid of the organic freedom found in traditional media, early critics dismissed it as a legitimate medium for the creation of art and design. Few recognized the birth of this new art form — one whose full potential has not yet been realized.**

*These pictures, he said sourly, not only resemble the notch patterns found on IBM cards, they have about the same amount of aesthetic appeal. They're cold and soulless, said the second as they walked away.*

*-Vincent**

*A character in the book *Becoming a Computer Artist*.
Chapter written by Professor Kathleen Gibson.

# Introduction

## Brief History of Digital Graphics

The origin of computer graphics can be dated to the early 1960s when researchers began work on the Sage system at the Massachusetts Institute of Technology (MIT). It was there that Ivan Sutherland developed the first interactive computer graphics system. Sketchpad, as it was called, allowed the cathode-ray tube (CRT) to be used as an electronic drafting board (Sutherland, 1963). Although sophisticated software for two-dimensional drafting, wireframe modeling, and meshed surfaces was rapidly being developed, the initial expense was prohibitive for commercial use.

For the design and construction industry, the 1970s was a decade of experimentation and software debugging. High expectations followed by economic disappointments created a fear in many design professionals which would last well into the next decade. Surveys of computer use in 1976 found less than 30 percent of architects and engineers involved with computing. Of those who utilized computers, their activities centered predominantly on project management tasks, i.e., accounting, design analysis, specification writing, and cost estimating, while firms retained manual methods for schematic

design and design development (Mileaf, 1982). Competition became the catalyst in the 1980s for many design firms to take another look at computer graphics. Mark Kates of the Walker Group states, "there was a pressure to get involved both from within and outside the industry" (Saitas, 1983). With more user-friendly software applications, lower hardware and peripheral costs, increased hardware performance, and a more computer-literate junior workforce, computer-aided design (CAD) gradually became widely accepted by the engineering and design communities.

Acceptance, however, was only the first step toward integrating computer graphics into the design process. Firms struggled with management, personnel, and cost issues. David Jordani of Ellerbe Associates noted that "computers created a fundamental change in the way we do our work, and created the need for a great deal of education of people at all levels of the organization" (Wagner & Mileaf, 1983, p. 41). Initially, many firms hired computer specialists and operators to input manually produced design sketches into the computer. Large firms initiated three shifts of CAD operators

**This book's ◀ definition of CAD**

*Computer-aided design (CAD) is the use of a computer for the creation, manipulation, analysis, and communication of an idea. This broad definition can include everything from drafting a plan, to writing a proposal via word processing software, to searching the World Wide Web for product information. This book narrows this large topic to focus exclusively on three-dimensional modeling, digital rendering and imaging, and animation.*

to use the equipment more effectively and reduce costs. While productivity quickly increased threefold at the construction document phase, computers still made little impact at earlier stages in the design process. In the early 1980s the computer was still seen by many in the design field as a production and documentation tool.

While many practitioners were trying to standardize computer-aided drafting, William Mitchell, then professor of architecture at UCLA and presently professor of architecture at MIT, was recommending more innovation and technical development. Mitchell discovered that the power of CAD lay not in documentation, but in extending current methods of thinking about design. In a relatively short time, designers began to recognize the visualization benefits of three-dimensional computer graphics. Unlike conventional two-dimensional drawings, wireframe models and animation provided a new method to study design solutions with greater realism than traditional media allowed. Architect Frank Gehry began using three-dimensional computer models to better visually communicate his ideas to the construction trades. Using software developed for the automotive and aerospace industries, Gehry's office digitally created a three-dimensional fish sculpture for the 1992 Olympic Village. Designing with digital tools ensured a high level of accuracy while reducing actual construction time and costs for the Olympic project (Novitski, 1992). Moreover, computer graphics proved not to be a liability for design creativity.

More sophisticated digital models have aided designers and engineers in both the analysis and the fabrication of materials, building systems, and simulated environments. Virtual reality, augmented reality, telepresence, videoconferencing, and the Internet are all new avenues for digital graphics. Although still quite crude, these technologies have enormous potential for both industry and education and will radically change how design is practiced in the next millennium.

## Digital Graphics and Visualization

Designers use many methods to communicate ideas to themselves and others. Sketching, modeling, and detailing are common practices throughout the design process. However, the one overriding skill needed to accomplish all these tasks is visualization. *Visualization* is the ability to create mental pictures which lead to the manifestation of a design solution. Not only does visualization assist the designer with communication, it also creates a method by which the designer is better able to understand, analyze, and implement design decisions (Figure 1-1). Visualization is the inner voice that asks, "What if?"

his dedication to *The Rival Ladies*. Here he speaks of a mass of confused thoughts from which his mind moves: ". . . the sleeping images of things towards the light, there to be distinguished, and then either chosen or rejected by the judgement" (Ghiseline, 1952, p. 80). For many, visualization becomes a mental tool to create and to solve problems.

**Figure 1-1** ◄
Visualization-
communication
model

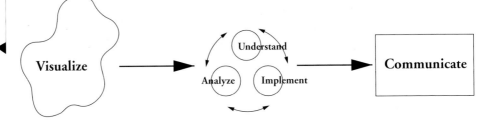

Visualization is not unique to those in the field of design. Scientist Albert Einstein relied on visual images to solve complex problems in physics. Describing his thought process, Einstein stated that ". . . elements in thought are certain signs and more or less clear images which can be voluntarily reproduced and combined. . . This combinatory play seems to be the essential feature in productive thought before there is any connection with logical construction in words or other kinds of signs which can be communicated to others" (Hanks, Belliston & Edwards, 1977, p. 72). Playwright John Dryden spoke of the creative process in

Techniques to improve visual thinking are numerous, each focusing on ways to free the mind from traditional patterns of thought. Exercises include daydreaming, gaming, brainstorming, synectics, and bionics. And what of computer graphics? Does digital technology contribute to visualization? William Mitchell, professor of architecture at MIT seems to think so. He states that computer graphics ". . . is the most exciting design medium I have ever gotten my hands on. It enables me to think in ways I can't do drawing on paper" (Wagner & Mileaf, 1983, p. 51). Take the schematic phase of designing, for example. The traditional approach forces one to work sequentially with two-dimensional, orthographic projections. Most designers begin with the plan, and then progress to the elevations and ceiling plane. However, the computer enables designers to work interactively in three-dimensional space, assessing the volumetric implications of every design decision. Working in virtual space benefits the designer's mental ability to holistically visualize and critically evaluate abstract ideas and relationships. The ability to cause designers to break free of rote habits and design methods which limit creative thinking is one of the greatest strengths of digital graphics.

Now this does not mean that manual techniques are ineffective and should be dismissed. Instead, it means that designers now have more options available for creative thinking and problem solving than ever before. However, more options do not necessarily mean better design solutions. Creativity is still a product of the human spirit; the computer remains a tool to assist designers in their creative explorations.

## Meaning and Use of Digital Graphics

How digital graphics or CAD is defined and thought of has a bearing on its use and benefit to the design and architectural community. In his book *Architectural Drawing: Options for Design*, Paul Laseau states, "It is the meaning . . . we assign [new digital tools] that will determine their contribution, and their role in design and drawing" (1991, p. 23). If that is true, what value do you place on digital graphics and CAD?

Several studies have focused on the relationship between CAD perceptions and its actual use in the design process. Introduced initially to the design community as a panacea for inert performance and stagnant profits, CAD was reserved for the final phases of the design process: working drawings, project administration, and redesign. Time, however, has proven CAD to have a broader contribution than initially expected. Case-study interviews with designers found that as CAD experience increased, designers used the technology for more qualified problem solving such as three-dimensional modeling. Somewhat surprisingly, firms also used CAD more exclusively for drawing and problem solving than for the expected information retrieval, redesign, calculations, specifications, and project administration (Hovmark & Norell, 1993). More importantly, research revealed a causal effect between the CAD attitudes of management and the actual performance by professional design staff. Administrators who viewed CAD as an electronic drafting tool derived little benefit from automating their offices, whereas managers who viewed the computer as a tool to improve team communication and problem solving received substantial benefit (Robertson & Allen, 1992). In light of these findings, the value placed on computer graphics is an important indicator of its effectiveness for design education and practice - not only for financial solvency and employment opportunities, but also for strengthening the development of visualization, problem-solving, and design communication skills.

## Integrating Digital Graphics Applications

As with traditional media, no one tool alone will accomplish every task. Imagine trying to complete a set of working drawings with watercolors and a paintbrush! The digital artist needs a collection of various software applications to match graphic strengths with individual need. Having only one CAD application at your disposal limits your creative thinking, which, in turn, leads to frustration. "Why won't the computer let me do this?" and "I can't be creative on the computer" are common statements of frustration resulting from choosing a software incompatible to the specific task. Assessing the different types of available graphic software and understanding what each has to offer is one of the primary goals of *Computer Visualization: An Integrated Approach for*

*Interior Design and Architecture.*
One of the most powerful features of all digital graphics is the ability to create a three-dimensional virtual environment. Chapter 2 focuses on the process of building three-dimensional objects, using sophisticated modeling procedures. Creating multiple wireframe perspective views is also a key element in this chapter. Chapter 3 uses a two-dimensional paint and imaging program to explore color relationships and placement. In addition to color manipulation, this chapter introduces the reader to the benefits of importing scanned images. Following previous lessons of digital color theory, Chapter 4 explores rendering materials and surface patterns in the third dimension. Chapter 5 experiments with lighting techniques, using shade, shadow, and high-

lights to lend a sense of realism to a digital model. Chapter 6 uses two-dimensional animation for dynamic multimedia presentations. Chapter 7 investigates advanced rendering and simulation opportunities for environmental design. And finally, Chapter 8 provides instruction for an animated walk-through of a virtual space. In all, the text demonstrates five different software applications. Some are used only for isolated exercises; however, many are shown with other software programs to provide an integrated view of computer graphics.

## Summary

Over 30 years ago, Ivan Sutherland created his first digital two-dimensional drawing. During the past three decades, the growth of computer-aided design has been a rapid, natural progression - -an evolution of drawing delineation. Just as stone, papyrus, mechanical pens, and T-squares before, the desire for better communication and documentation techniques led engineers and designers to the digital environment. Computer graphics happens to be the most recent advancement in a long history of drawing, a history which continues to evolve.

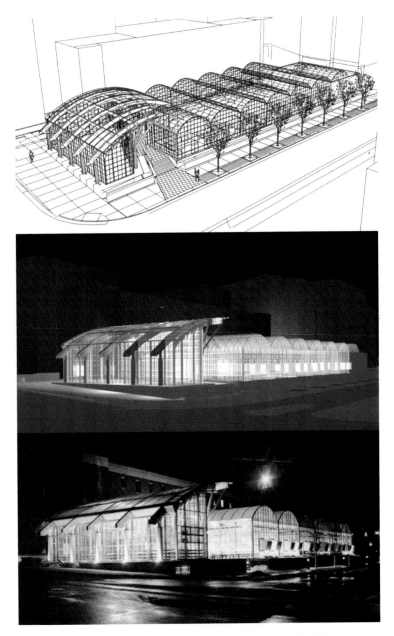

University of Wisconsin - Madison Instructional Greenhouse    **Flad & Associates**

# CONSTRUCTING A 3D DIGITAL MODEL

*2*

Any given design idea holds an infinite number of possibilities depending on what medium is used to express it. A painting expressed as a sculpture is indeed not the same as the original painting, but rather, the literal and figurative reflection of a new dimension of the original. By the same token, a set of two-dimensional (2D) drawings or a mental image, expressed as a three-dimensional (3D) digital model, has the ability to spark a new and potentially greater understanding of the original.

> *Vision and hearing are now the privileged sociable senses, whereas the other three [senses] are considered archaic sensory remnants with a merely private function, and they are suppressed by the code of culture.*
>
> *- Juhani Pallasmaa*

# Introduction

In the last part of the twentieth century, that which we perceive with our eyes has become the dominant way of knowing our world. At least that is part of the thesis of Juhani Pallasmaa (1996), the much admired Finnish polemicist and Professor of Architecture at Helsinki University of Technology. He suggests that "in Western culture, sight has generally been regarded as the noblest of the senses, and thinking itself is thought of in terms of seeing" (p. 6). Pallasmaa goes on to examine what he calls the "ocularcentric paradigm of our relation to the world and of our concept of knowledge . . . the privileging of vision" which he points out has been acknowledged and examined by philosophers as well as those who practice the art of architecture (pp. 8-9). The prominence of vision is intimately tied to the technological character of our society and as a result, we have developed a number of different systems to communicate, with graphics being one of the primary methods for expressing ideas.

The "visual communications language [graphics], incorporating text, images, and numeric information . . . may be called a 'universal language'. It is the natural method for humans to graphically communicate visual images of the mind. As far back as 1,200 B.C. cave drawings recorded and depicted aspects of the prehistoric human experience" (Bertoline, Wiebe, Miller, & Nasman, 1995, p. 9). The sidebar shows a historical time line of significant accomplishments in graphics. Designers tried many ways to visualize their creation before building it either by using two-dimensional sketches, three-dimensional drawings and models, or computer visualization. Digital media have elevated the visual senses to a new level.

For centuries architects and designers have used 3D models for thinking, visualizing, communicating, and predicting. In design, models are used for various purposes and are constructed as conceptual models, study models, and presentation models.

Conceptual models are for the designer in studying the physical relationship of ideas about mass, space, scale, and arrangement. The study [model] is a refinement of the conceptual model. It is used for more accurate representation of scaled detail or other physical elements, such as building openings and perhaps color. A presentation, or finished model, is a realistic, scaled representation of the completed project. It accurately portrays the designs through scale, materials, color, detail, and spatial and structural elements (Kilmer & Kilmer, 1992, pp. 572-573).

It was undoubtedly the desire to discover a new medium through which to express ideas that drove early computer pioneers to lay the foundation for 3D digital modeling. Unlike the computer itself, it is somewhat difficult to pinpoint the exact origin of 3D digital modeling. It was, in fact, the creative genius of several people working in concert that gave rise to the 3D digital modeling of today.

Some of the early work on 3D digital modeling was concentrated at the University of Utah (UU). In 1968, UU recruited Dave Evans, former director of engineering at Bendix Corporation's computer division from 1953 to 1962 and a University of California visiting professor at Berkeley, to form a computer science division. As a result of financial constraints, Evans was forced to narrow the focus of his program; he chose computer graphics as his focus and in doing so launched what would later be described as a golden period of intensive academic research in the field of computer graphics (Morrison, 1994, p. 38).

Since the early days in Utah, numerous people have contributed to the advancement of 3D digital modeling. As a result of their work and vision, 3D digital modeling has become as functional and accessible as any medium

## A Historical Time Line of Major Events in Drawings

| | |
|---|---|
| *2130 B.C.* | *Headless statues of Gudea, a Sumerian ruler* |
| *450 B.C.* | *Type of perspective drawings* |
| *1300-1500* | *Renaissance perspective and aerial perspective - Durer, da Vinci, Francesca, Alberti, and Brunelleschi* |
| *1790* | *Gaspard Monge - descriptive geometry* |
| *1820* | *William Farish - isometric drawing* |
| *1900* | *Standard practices* |
| *1960* | *Drafting machine* |
| *1963* | *Computer graphics, Ivan Sutherland - "Sketch Pad"* |
| *1970* | *CAD [2D drafting]* |
| *1985* | *Computer 3D modeling* |

*(Bertoline et al., 1995, p. 11)*

or tool in the arsenal of today's designers and architects. When making comparisons between a physical model and a computer model, there are at least three major considerations. The first category for comparison is the nature of models. The current computer model has much similarity with presentation models in the traditional physical modeling. It will be more beneficial for design educators and professionals to have CAD software which can build conceptual models to use in the early design stages. The second comparison is the modeling process. Computer modeling is an integrated and more comprehensive process than physical modeling. For example, the basic computer model can be the foundation for studying lighting and material, as well as being used for the final presentation model. The third category of comparison is modeling material. Physical modeling is the process of representing design ideas through the orderly use of clay, wood, foam, or other materials. Computer modeling is digital and more abstract without the physical satisfaction of the sense of touch.

The advantages of using 3D modeling versus 2D drafting are numerous. Three-dimensional models and their associated databases ease the transition from design to construction by reducing or eliminating the need for production of 2D drawings (See Figure 2-1). With the integration of computer technology, new architectural and interior design processes require the use of more intelligent and comprehensive drawings, such as sur-

**Now** *the computer* **can give us** *alternative ideas* **and can** ***participate*** *in the design process rather than* **be limited to what it could do in the past.**

face and solid models, which can contain important design information beyond the basic lines for dimension. The information may include such attributes as material specifications, construction demands, and visual representations.

Today, when we are designing, we are thinking beyond using CAD only for the 2D drafting. We are using 3D concepts to generate 3D drawings to represent the 3D environment. The process changes from drawing each plan of an object individually to the process of 3D sculpting by thinking in three dimensions initially and throughout the entire design process. Now the computer can give us alternative ideas and can participate in the design process rather than be limited to what it could do in the past.

▶ **TIP**

*For more information on the development of computer graphics, please see (Morrison, 1994), Becoming a Computer Animator, as well as other reference books (Betsky, 1997, p. 89).*

## A: Design to Construction, without 3D Computer Models

## B: Design to Construction with 3D Computer Models

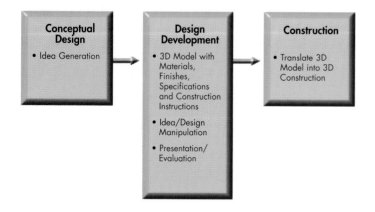

▶ **Figure 2-1**
Design to construction with and without 3D computer models

*"Just like a drawing, a model is an expression of the thought behind a design"* (Knoll & Hechinger, 1992, p. 8).

# Concepts

## 3D Modeling Environment

As with any new medium or tool, it is necessary to understand how to properly use the medium or tool in order to take full advantage of its potential. To do this, it is important to understand the fundamental difference between the 2D drawing surface and the digital 3D space. Traditionally, design drawings have been done within a 2D plan as defined by the X and Y axes, using 2D plans to represent the actual physical 3D environment. When we work on each plane separately - -for example, plan, section, or elevation – in an attempt to represent the totality of the real 3D environment, we can represent the depth of an object without actually being able to manipulate the object along what is referred to as the Z axis (the height).

*"I expect to see architects' growing use of 3D models instead of 2D documents. 3D will become standard operating procedure in all phases of architectural design before the year 2000"*

*(Joseph Brown, quoted in Amanzio, 1995, p. 8).*

Most of the time, design in 2D space requires mental visual ability to make the connection between 2D plans and the physical 3D environment. But not everyone is trained or has the ability to make this visual linkage. To understand how the Z axis affects a computer's interpretation of an object, it is first necessary to understand how the computer "sees" an object. A 2D object, a circle, for instance, can be described to the computer by the equation $X^2 \times Y^2 = R^2$ where the center of the circle is at the intersection of the X and Y axis, and points which satisfy the equation describe the circle. By adding the Z variable to the previous equation, $X^2 \times Y^2 \times Z^2 = R^2$, and assuming the same center point location, points which satisfy this equation form a sphere. Thus the additional axis provides depth information about the object. Using this information, the computer is then able to create a sophisticated 3D design space, which brings us one step closer to the type of interaction we experience in the physical 3D environment. Within this "3D design space" we can both manipulate an object along the Z axis as well and interact with multiple surfaces or planes of that object, all within the computer-generated 3D design space. There are several methods for creating 3D digital models. This chapter discusses the application of two of these methods in detail.

## Methods of 3D Modeling

When you use CAD software for visualizing design, the objects can be modeled in several ways. The most common processes can be categorized into two methods: extrusion and primitive modeling. The first method involves the creation of 2D shapes, which are extruded to add the third dimension: volume (Figure 2-2). This process, in terms of both thinking and technique, involves two steps. The first step is to think, view, and draw a 3D object as a 2D outline. The second step is to transform the 2D shapes into 3D entities by extruding each element to a certain height or thickness. Once an element is extruded, it becomes a 3D object for modification in 3D space. To work with this method, it is important to learn to visualize the relationship between 2D lines and 3D objects and to be able to make a 3D object from a 2D outline. This method shares the thinking strategy of conventional manual media. However, it differs in process by the fact that once the 3D objects are created, they can be moved, rotated, and otherwise manipulated in 3D space.

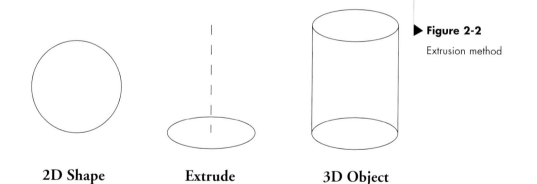

▶ **Figure 2-2**

Extrusion method

**2D Shape**　　　　**Extrude**　　　　**3D Object**

In using the primitive modeling (the second method), objects are modeled directly in a 3D design space as 3D forms. Working directly in 3D space has certain advantages because you can combine different modeling techniques to form complex objects. For example, if you are making a stool, the legs can be drawn using cylinders or other 3D primitives; the seat can be drawn as another cylinder. The thinking process is sculpturally based rather than the pictorial process of 2D creation. In Figure 2-3 part A, the diagram represents the 3D working space. Each arrow pointing to the diagram corresponds to a viewport in your 3D modeling program. In part B, the intersecting grids represent the *X*, *Y*, and *Z* coordinates of 3D space, with each grid corresponding to a particular axis. When the cube from part A and the grids from part B are combined to become part C, they illustrate how the coordinate system interacts with different views. This interaction is further illustrated in Figure 2-4. Part A shows what a teapot at 0,0,0 looks like from each of the different viewports. Part B demonstrates what happens in the viewport when the object is moved to 2,5,-3.

**Figure 2-3** ◀

3D working space

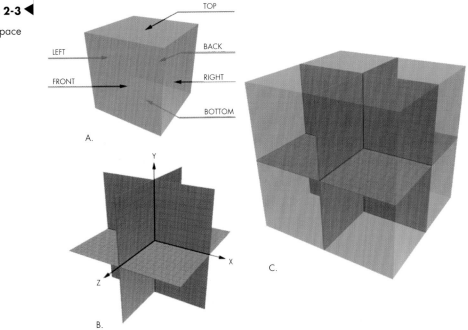

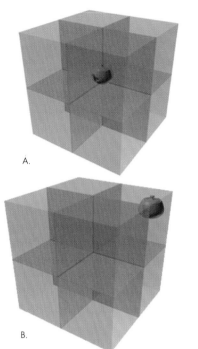

A.

B.

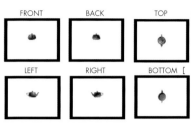

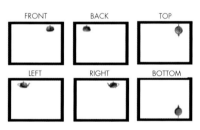

▶ **Figure 2-4**

The relationship between an objects position and the various viewports

▶ **TIP**

*Generally speaking, there are two strategies which are useful when selecting software based on available resources. You may choose to complete all the modeling and rendering processes within a single software package,*

*or you may construct the model using one software package and then transfer the file to another software package for rendering and further study.*

*Software packages are changing and improving in both their total*

*capabilities and the ease with which they read files from another package. A software package, which includes all capabilities from a 2D shape, 3D modeling, rendering, animation, and other functions, will be more*

*expensive. However, the transfer process can be complicated, and you should be sure that chosen packages and versions of applications are compatible before you make the purchase.*

## The Study of Perspective Drawings

"Around the year 450 B.C., the architects of the Parthenon, Ictinus and Callicrates, made a type of perspective drawing by foreshortening and converging parallel lines in their drawings. . . . From the 1400s on, the perspective technique has been the primary method used to communicate graphically" (Bertoline, 1995, pp.10, 13). Since then, perspective drawings have become the most effective communication format for the designer to represent reality. "The invention of perspective representation made the eye the center point of the perceptual world as well as of the concept of the self. Perspective representation itself turned into a symbolic form, one which not only describes but also conditions perception" (Pallasmaa, 1996, p. 7).

Perspective views portray a sense of space and depth to reflect the way we see real environments. They give an impression of depth as viewed from a particular position or viewpoint. Other ways of representing environments through more conventional means, such as diagrams, plans, elevations, or cross sections, do not have the unique advantage which is provided by the three-dimensional context of the surrounding setting.

In traditional manual representation of design ideas, perspective views were often completed at the end of the design process for final presentation of design ideas. If perspective drawings are closest in representing reality, why were they only created at the end of the design process? Because manual creation of perspective drawings is time consuming, and a perspective is a view from a single point. The design information that is portrayed is limited to one viewpoint for each drawing. Traditionally, a few key viewpoints that most completely represent the sense of space are chosen to be drawn and manually rendered for presentation. Digital modeling and rendering have changed the use of perspective viewing for design information. Computers will calculate and generate perspective views automatically based on the modeling information. Because of this, multiple perspective views can be chosen and used to aid in visualization of the environment long before the final drawings are produced.

## Modeling Elements

Harold Linton (1985) in his book *Color Model Environments* described several fundamental elements in three-dimensional design: theoretical, visual, organizational, structural, and plastic.

Included in the theoretical elements are the concepts of point, line, plane, and volume. These elements are often perceived in the designer's mind before they are given physical form. The visual elements - shape, size, color, and texture - are affected by the conditions under which we see them and establish the final appearance of a design. The organizational elements - position, orientation, space, and gravity - influence the overall structure and internal aspects of the visual elements. . . . Structural elements are important to our understanding of the construction of three-dimensional volumes. . . .The plastic elements, therefore, include any three-dimensional material that can be shaped by hand or tool and the visible relationships in arrangements of value gradations, contrasts, depth, and space (pp. 2-4).

No matter which medium is used, the principles and elements for three-dimensional design stay the same. Only the computer can be a new medium to effectively integrate the basic elements for creating three-dimensional design in the digital world. Figure 2-5 lists the computer features that relate each of those three-dimensional design elements.

| The Elements of Three-Dimensional Design | Specific Contents | CAD Approaches |
|---|---|---|
| Theoretical Elements | Point, Line, Plane, and Volume | Draw and Wireframe Construction Features |
| Visual Elements | Shape, Size, Color, and Texture | Shade and Rendering Features |
| Organizational Elements | Position, Orientation, Space, and Gravity | Navigation, UCS, and WCS Features |
| Structural Elements | Vertex, Edge, and Face | Modify and Solid Construction Features |

▶ **Figure 2-5**

CAD approaches for the three-dimensional design elements

## Modeling Construction

The objects we see, the environment we are in, all are the extension and transformation of basic **geometric primitives**, such as cubes, cylinders, triangular prisms, cones, and rectangular blocks. Francis D. K. Ching 1990, in his book *Drawing: A Creative Process*, explained the relationship between our physical environment and geometry, and he said "if we are able to break down what we see or envision into regular geometric solids, we can more easily draw them and study their relationships"(p.162). Professor Ching (1990) theorizes that there are three basic forms for constructing many objects: additive forms, subtractive forms, and complex forms. Additive forms are the process of a basic unit which can be expanded in all directions. In the subtractive-forms process, "we use the solid-void relationship between form and space as the generating principle for what we create." When constructing complex forms, we can work in both an additive and a subtractive manner (p.164).

In computer modeling, many features share the same concept with the manual modeling concept, only they are represented differently: for instance, the **Boolean Operation**, which is combining two solid objects (additive forms), subtracting one from another (subtractive forms), or determining intersecting areas between overlapping solid objects (complex forms). In the 3D modeling process, most elements can be constructed by using geometric primitives, which are the basic solid or geometric shapes that can be used as building blocks for modeling in 3D space. Geometric primitive shapes can be used individually or combined to form complex objects. Figure 2-6 illustrates the process of creating a wall and window model using the Boolean Operation.

**TIP ◄**

*The following are some specific terms that have to be understood before modeling starts. Edges are the lines that represent the boundary between two faces of an object. Faces are areas of uniform or gradually changing lightness and are always bounded by edges. Both edges and faces can be curved. Vertices are the places or corners where more than two edges meet.*

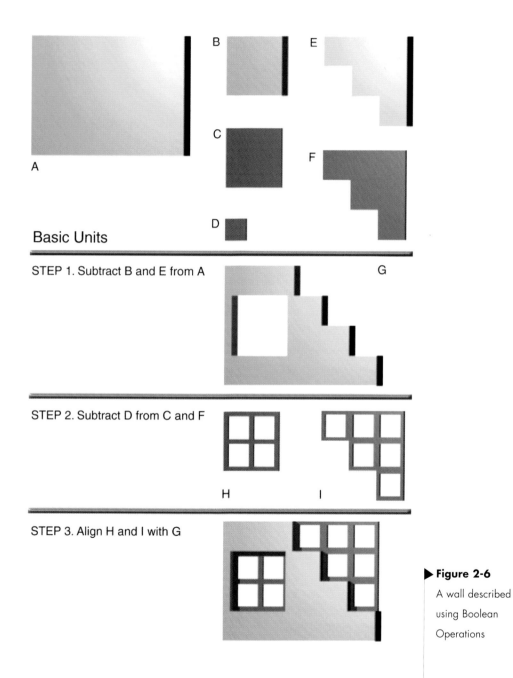

Basic Units

STEP 1. Subtract B and E from A

STEP 2. Subtract D from C and F

STEP 3. Align H and I with G

▶ **Figure 2-6**

A wall described using Boolean Operations

# Cognition

Computer modeling not only requires a new creation and thought process, but learning new concepts and terms specific to 3D modeling. It is important to keep in mind that different software packages may explain the same concepts using different terminology. We are introducing the following concepts and terms in a general sense to help the reader understand the concepts rather than memorize specific software explanations.

## Conceptual Process

### Using Manual Sketching for Preparation of Computer Modeling

Manual sketching has the advantage of representing our design ideas faster and more easily in the conceptual design stage. After we have sketched our ideas on paper, we begin to visually analyze them. Upon completion of our analysis, we begin to consider how we might use the computer to represent our design solution. Then we evaluate the available computer tools and decide which are most appropriate for the given task.

### From Computer Experimentation to Modeling

In some cases, it is useful to begin the conceptual phase of a project directly on the computer. As is the case with manual sketching, for computer sketching to be effective, you should become familiar and comfortable with the available tools. To do this, it is necessary to begin with free experimentation, using as many of the available tools as possible. The first time you apply a tool to a 3D object, the results are generally unpredictable. However, the more you use and experiment with the various tools, the easier it becomes to achieve a consistent and predictable result. It is the knowledge gained from this type of unstructured experimentation that will ultimately result in the ability to create by using only the computer.

## Planning a Modeling Strategy

In order for the computer to be an effective 3D design tool, it is essential to understand the computerized process by which we design using the computer. Since the nature of the CAD is hierarchical, it is essential that very careful consideration be given to even the earliest stages of the CAD process. Indeed, it is the 3D model which forms the foundation upon which all additional elements (rendering, animation, etc.) will be built. Be sure to select appropriate modeling types for different tasks. A skeletal description of 3D objects is created by a form of modeling called a **wireframe model.** No surfaces are drawn, only points, lines, and curves. Wireframe modeling is good if you do not need to do further rendering. **Surface model** is a form of modeling in which planes and surfaces are defined. The surfaces are faceted using a polygonal mesh. **Solid model** is yet another type of modeling in which 3D forms contain mass and can be combined, subtracted, and edited.

After you select the appropriate modeling type, set up an effective work environment, which is critical to 3D modeling. **Units** are the segments of measurement for reference and for scaling of drawings or measuring the distance between two coordinate points. Units can be measured in scientific, decimal, engineering, and architectural units or fractions. Angles can be measured in degrees, minutes, seconds, grads, radians, and surveyor's units. **Limits** create an invisible drawing boundary that helps to fit the drawing to paper at the chosen scale. "**Layers** are the basic organizational structure of most CAD systems and allow selective filtering, viewing, sharing, and plotting of graphic information" (Sanders, 1996, p. 264). **Drawing aids** help you to draw with precision and accuracy. The **grid** is a pattern of dots that helps to align objects and visualize distance. The **snap**, when active, restricts the cursor to movement between set intervals. **Elevation** is the location of an object, point, or line on the Z axis (the altitude above plans). The current elevation at the time something is drawn determines this location. **Thickness** or **height** is the distance an object is extruded above or below its elevation. It is a specific measure between opposite sides.

## Navigating 3D Space

### Coordinate Systems

Coordinate systems are familiar to many people from their high school mathematics classes for plotting points and graphing. Coordinate systems in 3D modeling are also used for placing points in space. The coordinate system used for 3D modeling is defined by axes and the point of intersection of axes is the origin, where measurement begins (0,0,0). Many CAD software programs use a **cartesian coordinate system**, and the origin is the point where the values of X and Y are both zero. You can draw in both positive and negative coordinates. The numbers, or coordinates, marking location along the axes (0,0,0) are based on the chosen unit of measurement. Often in design, an architectural scale of inches and feet is used with the smallest measurable distance dependent upon the size of the finished drawing. The drawing can be oriented in any chosen way in the axis system; however, it is most common to have the $X$ and $Y$ axes define the horizontal plane, or plan view, for the drawing and the $Z$ axis to keep track of the vertical location or height from the ground plane. AutoCAD uses World and User-Coordinate systems as a way of changing the current drawing plane. This is discussed in detail in the Applications section.

### Navigational Tools

**Zooming** is the process of reducing and increasing the viewing area of a drawing. Zooming is necessary because sometimes an entire drawing needs to be seen to complete the work, and at other times only sections need to be seen in order to add details to a piece. Individual software packages have different techniques for using zoom commands, but it is necessary to learn to use these features. The three most common navigational tools - **zoom, pan,** and **rotate** – can be found in any 3D modeling package.

## Limitations of File Size

Unlike the familiar word processing files, which can fit easily onto a standard floppy disk, 3D drawing and modeling files can become so large that they require special storage media. Although several things contribute to the size of a given 3D file, the most important to consider is the number of 3D objects and their level of complexity. Each 3D model in a given scene has a certain number of faces that compose its surface. The smoother a surface must appear, the more faces are necessary. Similarly, the more complex and detailed a surface, the more faces are needed. In fact, it is these faces which account for a significant portion of the size of a given 3D file. Given this, it is possible to plan ahead and eliminate unnecessary faces, thus reducing the size of a file.

There are many methods to reduce the drawing size; two approaches are explained below. First, if you know that certain objects will always be far away in the background or greatly obscured by another object in the scene, those objects can be modified so that the minimum number of faces are used. The resulting objects are not as smooth as some of the more prominent objects in the scene; however, the reduction in file size is significant. Second, bitmap images are used in place of complex geometry. For instance, if your 3D image requires a tall building with many windows, and the building is merely part of a distant skyline, a simple rectangle can be covered with a digital image of windows, creating the desired illusion of complexity without actually altering the geometry or creating additional faces. However, if the building is a prominent object in the foreground of the scene and we will be looking through the windows to the interior, it is necessary to modify the geometry of the building to create windows. This approach will create an enormous number of additional faces and increases the size of the file.

# Applications

As was mentioned earlier, there are several methods of digital modeling and rendering. In this chapter we demonstrate two of the most common methods. In the first method, we begin with 2D lines, extrude to 3D entities, and transfer into a 3D modeling space. The second method is direct modeling in a 3D space. We build the same table, using both methods. For method 1, we will use Autodesk's 3D Studio (3DS R4) for the entire process, taking advantage of its total modeling and rendering capabilities. For method 2, we will use Autodesk's AutoCAD and 3D Studio Max (3D Max) for modeling directly in 3D space and transfer the file to 3DS R4 and 3D Max for future study.

## Using 3DS R4 with the "Extrude" Concept to Model a Table

Before we begin it is best to know a little bit about the basics of the software package that we are using. The 3D Studio package consists of five modules, each with a separate function within the program:

**Figure 2-7** ◀

Program pull-down
menu

**2D Shaper** [F1]: This is used for the creation of 2D polygons that can later be modified into 3D objects.

**3D Lofter** [F2]: Shapes created in the 2D Shaper module are imported and are given three-dimensionality, turning the shapes into objects.

**TIP** ◀

*In this book, 3D space refers to a three-dimensional modeling interface on the computer screen, and 3D environment refers to a physical surrounding in the reality.*

**3D Editor** [F3]: This is used to modify the polygons as complete objects. Materials, lights, and cameras for rendering a still frame can be set in this module. Also 3D Editor can be used to create simple 3D objects.

**Keyframer** [F4]: This is used to produce animation, employing the objects, cameras, lights, and materials added in 3D Editor. Keyframer can also be used for editing lights, cameras, and materials.

**Materials Editor** [F5]: This is used to create and edit the surface materials to be assigned to objects in the 3D Editor (Figure 2-7).

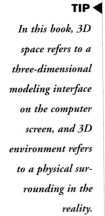

```
Program  Network
2D Shaper     F1
3D Lofter     F2
3D Editor     F3
Keyframer     F4
Materials     F5
BROWSER       F6
CAMERA/PREVU  F7
IK            F8
KEYSCRIPT     F9
DOS Window    F10
Text Editor   F11
PXP Loader    F12
```

Modules are used at different times during the modeling and rendering process depending upon their function. The following is a very basic outline of the progression of 3D modeling using 3D Studio:

1. Create a 2D representation of what you are modeling, using the 2D Shaper.
2. Loft the pieces of the model to appropriate heights, using the 3D Lofter, giving them the 3D volume, and turning them into objects.
3. Arrange the lofted pieces, which are now objects in the 3D space of the 3D Editor.

Once modeling is complete, rendering takes place by switching between the Materials Editor and the 3D Editor to edit and assign materials, lighting, and camera views. As most computer users have learned the hard way, it is important to save your work often as you progress. And 3D Studio is unique in the fact that the different modules act as separate programs for the purpose of saving and retrieving work. This means that work done in each module used a different file specification and must be saved in that module. For example, the 2D Shaper saves the shapes as filename.shp, and the 3D Editor creates filename.3ds files. If you make changes in both the 3D Editor and the 2D Shaper, you must save your work in both modules.

### Drawing Setup

Before we begin the modeling, there are some steps to follow to set up the drawing space. To set the units for interior and architectural modeling, it is best to use architectural units of measure for consistency with other drawings and measurements. To set the units, click on the following menus: **VIEWS\Unit Setup\Architectural**, then click on **OK** on the Measurement Unit Selection panel to keep the denominator 100 and 1 unit = 1 inch (Figure 2-8).

▶ **Figure 2-8**

Units setup panel

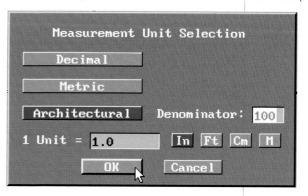

## Drawing Aids

There are several drawing aids available to ensure accuracy in building forms. To set the drawing aid, click on the following menus: **VIEWS\Drawing Aids**. The ideal snap spacing is dependent upon the size of the objects being modeled and the required precision. The spacing can be modified at any time during the process. For the table model, type **1"** for X and then click on the Y in order to copy the value to Y and Z for Snap Spacing.

For this exercise, set the Grid Spacing at **6"** by typing **6"** in for X and clicking on the Y to copy the value. The values for the Grid Extent Start and End points depend upon the size of the finished drawing. For this exercise, type **0** as the Grid Extent Start point and **12'** as the Grid Extent End. The angle snap can remain at 10 degrees for now but can be changed when more precision is necessary. Then click on **OK** (Figure 2-9).

Once the values for the drawing aids are set, they need to be turned on in every viewpoint where they will be used. This can be done whenever a viewpoint is active by clicking on the following: **VIEWS\Use Snap\Use Grid\Use Angle Snap.**

**Figure 2-9** ◀

Configuring render output panel

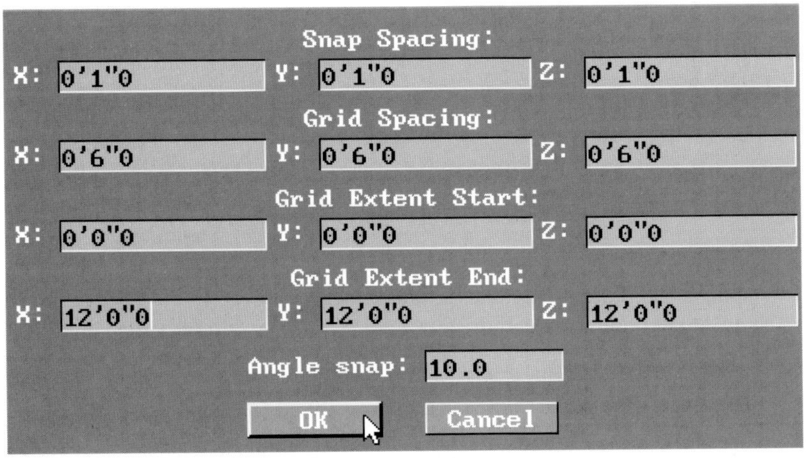

| Snap Spacing: | | |
|---|---|---|
| X: 0'1"0 | Y: 0'1"0 | Z: 0'1"0 |
| **Grid Spacing:** | | |
| X: 0'6"0 | Y: 0'6"0 | Z: 0'6"0 |
| **Grid Extent Start:** | | |
| X: 0'0"0 | Y: 0'0"0 | Z: 0'0"0 |
| **Grid Extent End:** | | |
| X: 12'0"0 | Y: 12'0"0 | Z: 12'0"0 |

Angle snap: 10.0

OK        Cancel

## Zooming

Before we begin, it is also important to know how to use the zoom commands. There are several icons in the lower right-hand corner of the screen that will be used throughout the modeling process (Figure 2-10):

Zoom extent icon: Brings all the drawing into the boundaries of the viewports.

Zoom in icon: Magnifies the active view by 50 percent.

Zoom out icon: Displays 50 percent more of the drawing in the active viewport.

Window zoom icon: Zooms the active viewport to a defined area.

Full screen toggle: Changes between four windows, and only one window shows on the screen. An active button is red.

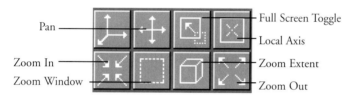

Pan ——
Full Screen Toggle
Local Axis
Zoom In ——
Zoom Extent
Zoom Window ——
Zoom Out

▶ **Figure 2-10**
Navigation tool in 3D Studio R4

## Beginning the Table Drawing

We are now ready to begin the modeling process in the 2D Shaper module. This can be entered by selecting it from the program's menu or by pressing the [F1] key. At this point in the modeling process, all the objects are drawn as 2D lines and shapes, so it is important to examine and understand the relationship between 2D lines and shapes and 3D objects.

To begin, it is helpful to draw the objects and spaces in the Top view (look at the object from top down), since it is a common 2D representation of space. From this viewpoint, we will draw the shapes in 2D Shaper by creating a series of 2D closed figures or polygons. Then we transfer individually into 3D Lofter for the addition of 3D volume (Figure 2-11).

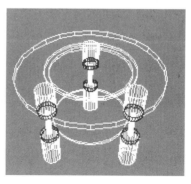

▶ **Figure 2-11**
Wireframe display of the finished table model for method 1

In the plan view, the table in this exercise looks like a series of related circles, varying in placement and diameter. After lofting the objects, we can move them around in the 3D Editor program, but we will create the lines relative to one another from the Top view. This will make it easier to piece together objects since only the relative heights need to be added later.

First, draw the frame to create the whole tabletop as a solid cylinder. Then subtract the center hole and make the space for the glass to sit on.

In the 2D Shaper program, click on the following commands: **CREATE\*Circle*. You will then be prompted to enter the center point for the circle. Place the cursor near the center of the drawing (X: 6'0"; Y: 6'0") and click to enter the center of the circle. The computer will then prompt you to the radius of the circle. Watch the coordinate display at the top of the screen as you move the mouse and cursor to the right, and click when the display reads *1'4"* (Figure 2-12).

Using the same center of the first circle, draw a second smaller circle, and click on the top coordinate display radius at 10". Now draw the third circle, starting with the same center as the previous two circles, and click on the radius as *0'9"* (Figure 2-13).

Then you may use the Zoom Window to enlarge the working area. The first circle is outside the table frame. The second is the edge of the glass, and the third is the edge of the hole. The space between the second and third circles is the ledge on which the glass will be sitting.

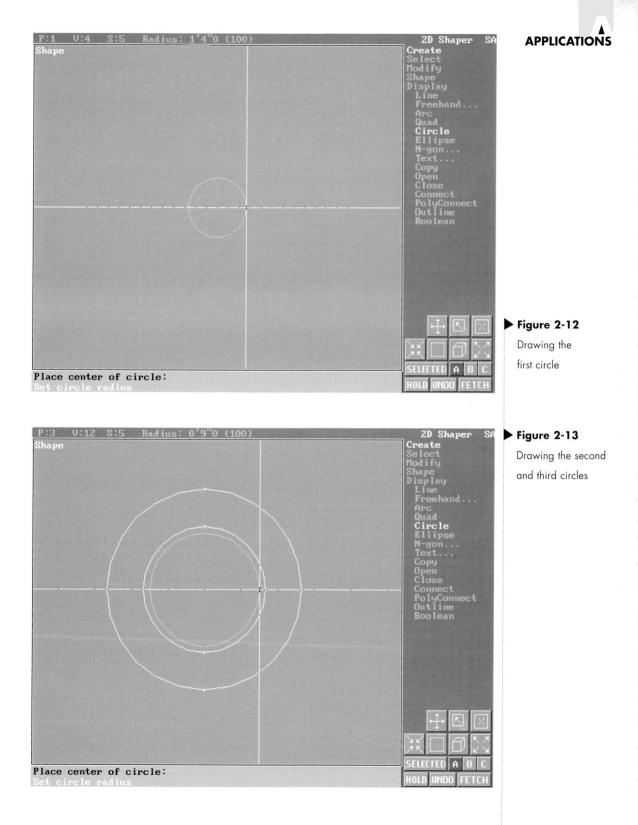

▶ **Figure 2-12**

Drawing the

first circle

▶ **Figure 2-13**

Drawing the second

and third circles

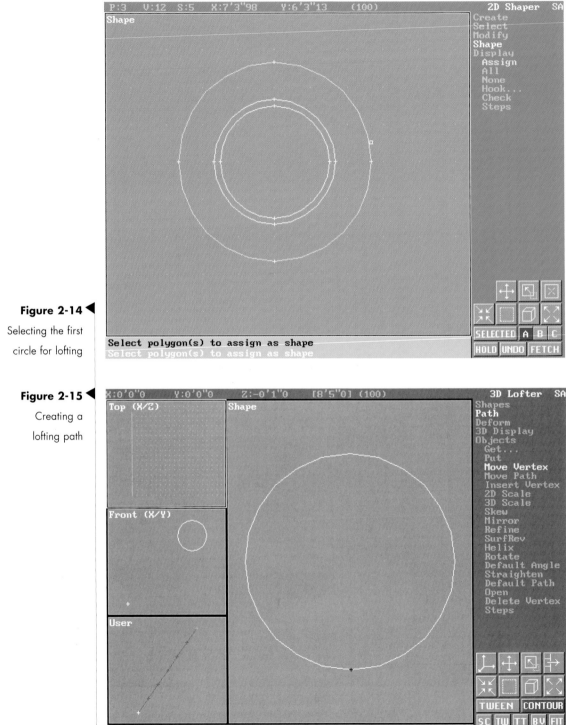

**Figure 2-14** ◀

Selecting the first circle for lofting

**Figure 2-15** ◀

Creating a lofting path

You are now ready to extrude or give thickness (depth, height, or volume) to shapes to turn them into objects. Each piece of an object or drawing that will be given a different material or that has a specific thickness should be lofted individually. They will each be considered a separate object for specific modification. The pieces or individual sections are chosen from the shapes that were just drawn in 2D Shaper before you enter the 3D Lofter module. This is done by clicking on **SHAPE\\*Assign*, and on the larger circle. When you click on the object, it will turn yellow, indicating that it is currently chosen. Clicking again on the object will turn off its current assignment (Figure 2-14).

Now enter the 3D Lofter module either by choosing it from the program's pull-down menu or by keying [F2].

The currently assigned shape is imported into this module by clicking on the following commands: **SHAPE\\*Get\\Shaper*. The current shape, in this case the large circle, should now appear in the viewports. What you see in the viewports along with the circle is a path. The path indicates the height to which the object will be lofted when the object is created. Before you create the shape, you must set the path to the desired height of the object. To accomplish this, first make the Top viewport active by clicking on it. Turn on Snap and Grid for this viewport to ensure accuracy. The cursor should currently be a +. Hitting the [Tab] key will change the cursor between +, –, and |. Hit the [Tab] key until the cursor is the vertical line. This allows things to be changed in only this direction. This is also helpful for ensuring that the path is precise. Now, to change the path, click on the following: **PATH\\*Move Vertex*. Then click on the top vertex of the path (the vertices are indicated by small crosses along the line). With the cursor set vertical, the path moves only higher or lower. Set the path to the desired thickness of the shape. In this case set the path at *1″* to make the frame top *1″* thick (Figure 2-15).

You can now create the object by clicking on the following: **OBJECTS\\*Make*. At this time, we are prompted to name the object. We type in a name that makes sense to us so that when it is time to assign the materials, we can choose the objects by name. For example, we could name this object **topsupport**, indicating the frame section of the tabletop, and then click on the **Create** button on the bottom part of the panel (Figure 2-16).

▶ **Figure 2-16**

Naming object panel

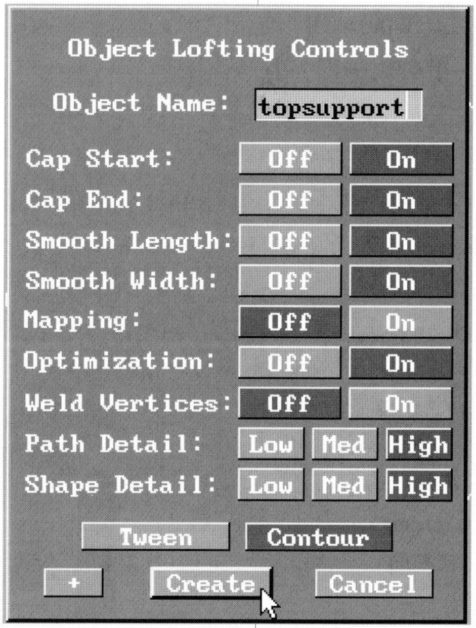

**Object Lofting Controls**

| | | |
|---|---|---|
| Object Name: | topsupport | |
| Cap Start: | Off | On |
| Cap End: | Off | On |
| Smooth Length: | Off | On |
| Smooth Width: | Off | On |
| Mapping: | Off | On |
| Optimization: | Off | On |
| Weld Vertices: | Off | On |
| Path Detail: | Low | Med | High |
| Shape Detail: | Low | Med | High |

Tween    Contour

+    Create    Cancel

**TIP** ◄

*You may use Full Screen Toggle to enlarge the top view to make sure the three circles have three different sides.*

Go back to 2D Shaper by pushing the [F1] key. Make sure **SHAPE\\*Assign*** is highlighted. Click on the yellow circle to turn *off* the selection. Click on the middle circle, and then the [F2] key into 3D Lofter. Select **SHAPE\\*Get\\Shaper***, and a panel will appear to verify your decision. Just click on the **Yes** button.

Then click on **PATH\\*Move Vertex*** (for better accuracy you may enlarge the Top viewport). Turn off the User Snap features from the Views panel to allow you to make **1/2"** thickness. Click on when you see **Z:0'0" 50** on the top of the screen; then click on **OBJECT\\*Make*** and type **tophole1** for the object name. Finally, click on the **Create** button.

Now it is time to go back to the 2D Shaper again. Click on the third circle and make sure to turn off the second circle. Make the third circle **2"** thick and name it **tophole2**. Then move into 3D Editor by using the [F3] key to get in.

Click on **MODIFY\\*Object\\Move***, then move the second circle to match the surface of the larger circle (Figure 2-17). Click on **CREATE\\*Object\\Boolean*** and activate the Top view.

**Figure 2-17** ◄

Moving objects in 3D Editor

**TIP** ◄

*By using Top viewport, change the thickness and watch the top coordinate display stop at Z: 0'0"50.*

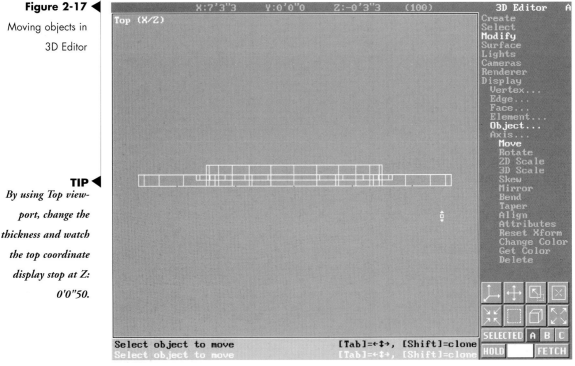

▶ **Figure 2-18**

Wireframe
display of the
finished table top

Select the larger circle for the first selection, and then click on the middle-sized circle. The Boolean Operation panel will appear. Make sure the Subtraction and the Weld Elements are highlighted, and then click on **OK**. Repeat this process to subtract the smaller circle from the larger one. Now the top frame part of the table is complete (Figure 2-18).

It is time to go back to the 2D Shaper to finish the rest of the table. In the 2D Shaper environment, all three circles can still be used. The middle-sized circle can be used for glass, and the smaller-sized circle can be the inner support circle of the table. For the legs, start to draw one circle, and then using the **CREATE\Copy** command, duplicate the other two. After you copy them to the appropriate position, you can use the **MODIFY\ Polygon\Move** command to move them more precisely (Figure 2-19). You can use the same procedure to create the center support piece for each leg, and then copy the small circle into the center of

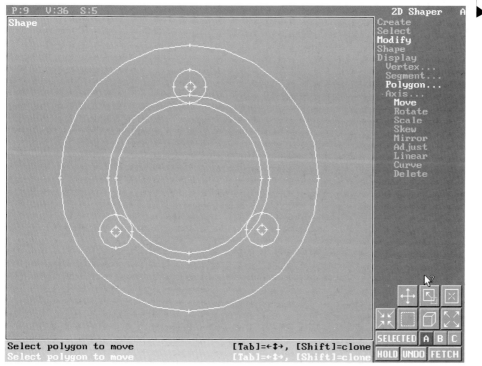

▶ **Figure 2-19**

Copying table legs

each leg. The next step is to click on **SHAPE\\Assign** to click on the second largest circle, which is going to be glass. Use **PATH\\Move Vertex** in 3D Lofter to make the glass have **1/2"** thickness. Then make the object called **glass** and make the third largest circle, named **centersupt,** with **1/2"** thickness.

The next step is to assign the three legs. Because the legs are divided by top and bottom parts, you need to use the same circle twice. The bottom can be named **legB** for the object name, and change the vertex to **8"** for thickness. The top part can be named **legT**, with **6"** for the thickness. Then assign **6"** for height to the center-support cylinder of each leg. The last step is to create the metal part of each leg by using the same circles for the three legs. You can give **1"** for the height. Now by hitting the [F3] key, you can switch to 3D Editor environment.

In 3D Editor, you will see four separate windows or viewports: Top, Front, Left or Right, and User. Only one window is active for editing at any given time, and the active window is marked with a thicker border. Any viewport can be activated by clicking within its boundary.

The user viewport is a perspective view chosen and created by the computer. You notice that the table is oriented incorrectly, and in the user view the table is on its side. To reorient the drawing you need to rotate all objects. Since the entire table needs to be rotated by the same amount, it can be rotated with one set of commands. To rotate the table, first set the Angle Snap to **On** in the viewport you are working in the **VIEWS\\Angle Snap**. Then click on **SELECT\\All**; at this point the entire table should be red, indicating that it has all been selected. There is a button labeled **Selected** in the lower right hand corner of the screen. Click on the button, turning it red (indicating "on") to make sure that the following commands will affect everything that is selected, in this case the entire table.

**TIPS** ◀ *You may need to click on the Zoom Extent icon to replace the table in all windows.*

*The first appearance on the screen may be only a partial view of the object, so you need to use Zoom Window and the Full Screen Toggle icon to make a large area for your task.*

*You may start to move the center cylinder first in the top position.*

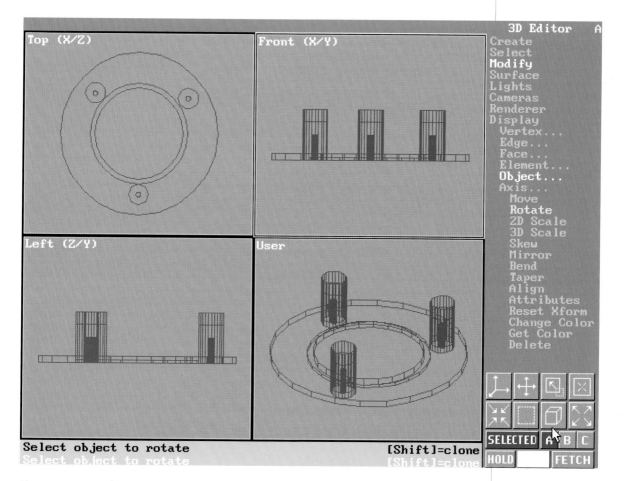

▶ **Figure 2-20**

Table position

after rotation

We are now ready to rotate the drawing by clicking on **MODIFY\\*Object*\\*Rotate*. You may need to rotate the table in both Front and Top viewports. Click on the table. When you move the mouse, the table rotates and the angle of rotation is indicated in the display at the top of the screen. When the table is standing correctly, it should read a **90°** rotation. Click to set the table into place. The table should look like Figure 2-20.

The objects are imported and scaled relative to their placement in 2D Lofter. The individual objects (now 3D) must now be moved to their appropriate height relative to one another to construct the finished project. Click on **MODIFY\\*Object*\\*Move*.

In the Front viewport, you may start first to move the three smallest cylinders in the center in order to place them on top of the bottom part of the leg. Then move the top part of the leg

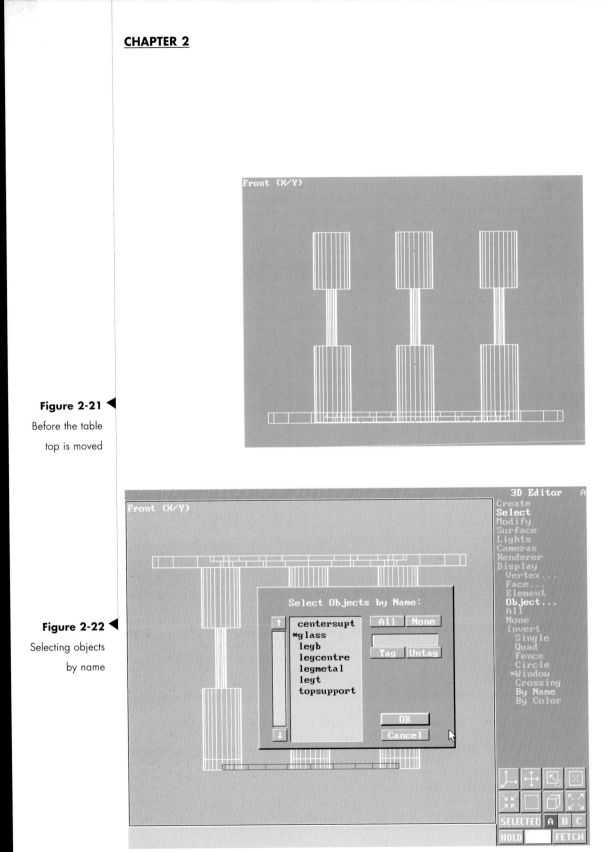

**Figure 2-21**
Before the table
top is moved

**Figure 2-22**
Selecting objects
by name

on top of those smallest cylinders. Then you can put the frame in place and then the glass. The last piece to be positioned is the center support section (Figure 2-21). One easy way to identify objects in a complex layering environment is by using **SELECT\\*Object*\\*Name*** to identify the exact location of the object you want to modify (Figure 2-22).

We are now ready to choose the view of the table that we want for the perspective views. This is done by the creation of a camera, or multiple cameras for multiple views. To create a camera, click on the following menu items: **CAMERAS\\*Create***. You will then be prompted for the placement of the camera. In the Top view, choose a spot in the active viewport (the program will not accept placement in "User viewport") and click to set the camera. Then you will be asked to place the target. Click on the section of the object where you want to point the camera. (At this point, do not be overly concerned with placement because it is easily changed.) A menu will appear to set up the camera. The default selections will work for now, so simply click on ***Create*** (Figure 2-23).

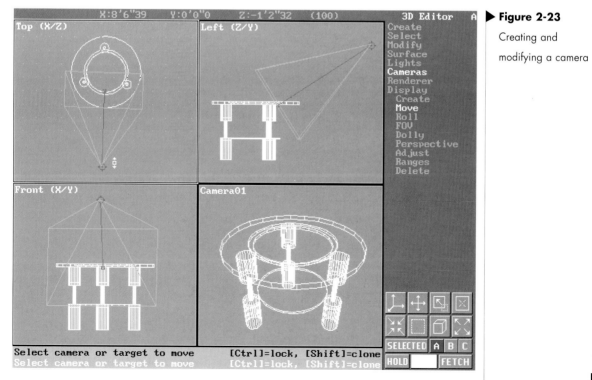

▶ **Figure 2-23**

Creating and modifying a camera

**Figure 2-24** ◀

Positioning a

camera

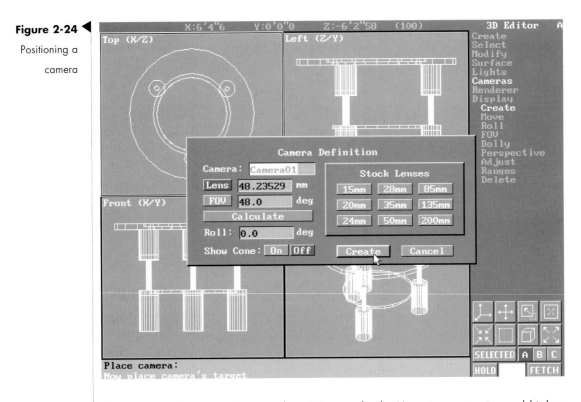

To see where the camera is currently pointing, make the User viewport active and hit key [C]. This will change the user view to the camera view. If you have more than one camera, you will be prompted to choose the camera view that you want to see. Often, the view is not what you want to see; sometimes the camera is not pointing at any part of the object. To change the view, choose **CAMERAS\Move** (Figure 2-24).

**TIP** ◀
*Changing the cursor with the [Tab] key to restrict the movement to one direction will help with the placement.*

The table is now properly scaled and modeled. It is ready for material selection, lighting, and any other desired rendering effects.

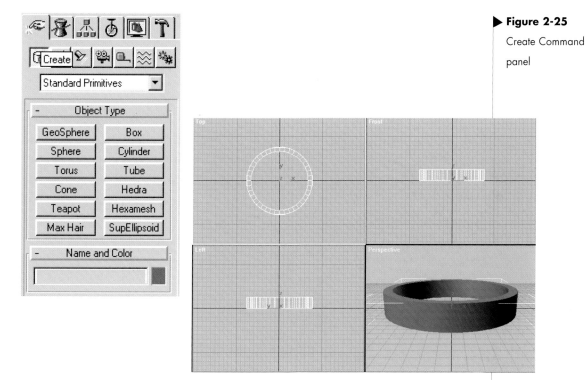

▶ **Figure 2-25**

Create Command

panel

## Using 3D Max to Model the Table in a 3D Space

▶ **Figure 2-26**

Initial steps for

creating a tube

The first step after starting 3D Max is to set up the units. This is done by going to the **VIEW\Units Setup** inside the **Units Setup** panel. Choose *"US Standard"*, select *"Feet W/Fractional Inches"*, and set the accuracy to *1/2*; then click on **OK**. To begin drawing the table, click on the **CREATE** icon to display the **CREATE** panel (see Figure 2-25). Make sure the **Standard Primitives** menu is showing and select *Tube*. In the Top viewport, click on the center and drag the mouse outward. Release the mouse button, drag inward, and click once; then drag upward and click once more. After the tube is finished, right-click in the Top viewport to turn off the tube command (see Figure 2-26). At this stage it is not important to be accurate with the tube's dimensions; we will set them precisely in the next step.

▶ **TIP**

*Use the Zoom Extent*

*or Zoom Out to fill*

*the viewports with*

*your object.*

Make sure the object is selected (highlighted in white) and click the **MODIFY** icon which is next to the **CREATE** icon. Copy the settings for the frame of the tabletop from Figure 2-27. From the Top viewport, move the frame of tabletop so that the axis icon (X and Y in red) in the center of the object is aligned with an intersection of the background grid. This action provides a reference center point for the next cylinder. Click on the **CREATE** icon and select **Cylinder**. In the Top viewport, click in the center of the frame to begin the new cylinder. Click and drag outward; then release the mouse button and move the lines upward. Click to set the height. Right-click in the top viewport (active viewport) to turn off the cylinder tool. Make sure that the new cylinder is selected and click on the **MODIFY** icon to enter the precise settings for the cylinder. Copy the settings for the cylinder from Figure 2-28. In the Top viewport, position the cylinder so that it has the same center point as the frame. In the Front viewport, position the cylinder so that it is intersecting the frame at the halfway point (see Figure 2-29). Before we subtract the cylinder to create the groove for the glass, copy the

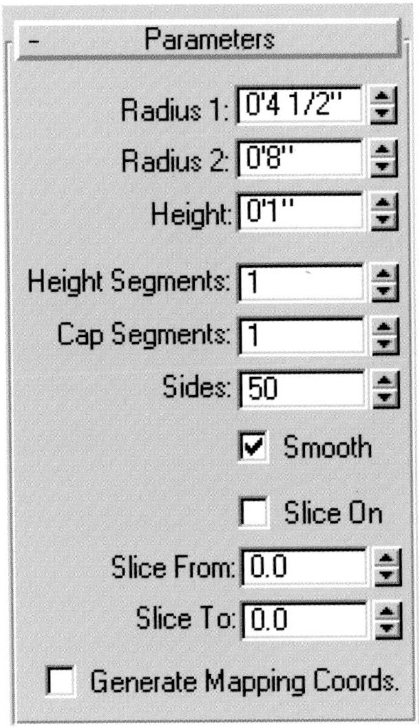

**Figure 2-27** ◀

Settings for the frame of the table top

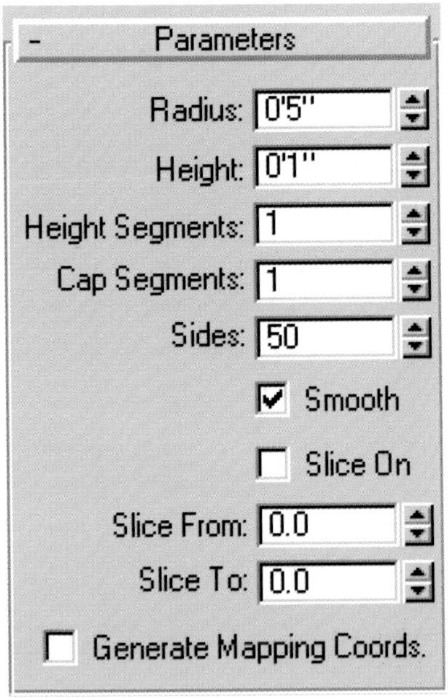

**Figure 2-28** ◀

Settings for the cylinder

**Parameters**

Radius 1: 0'4 1/2"
Radius 2: 0'8"
Height: 0'1"
Height Segments: 1
Cap Segments: 1
Sides: 50
☑ Smooth
☐ Slice On
Slice From: 0.0
Slice To: 0.0
☐ Generate Mapping Coords.

**Parameters**

Radius: 0'5"
Height: 0'1"
Height Segments: 1
Cap Segments: 1
Sides: 50
☑ Smooth
☐ Slice On
Slice From: 0.0
Slice To: 0.0
☐ Generate Mapping Coords.

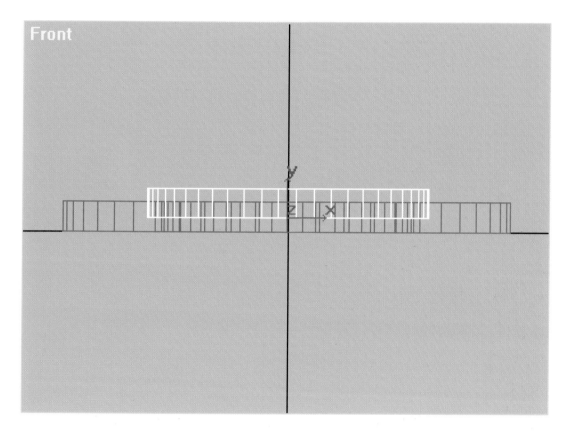

Front

▶ **Figure 2-29**

Positioning cylinder
for subtraction

**Figure 2-30** ◀

Table frame after

subtraction

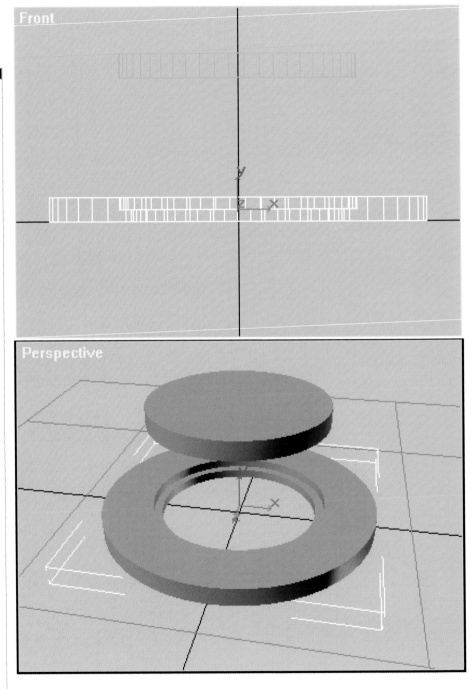

cylinder, which is already in the correct position, and use it as the glass. To do this, click the constrain to the **Y** axis button on the top menu bar and in the Front viewport. Hold down the shift key and drag the cylinder upward. In the Clone Option panel, type the name **glass** for the copy of the cylinder and click **OK**. To begin the subtraction, click on the original cylinder to select it, click on the **CREATE** icon, and select **Compound Objects** from the dropdown menu. From the Compound Objects panel, click on **Boolean**. In the Boolean panel, select **Subtract (B minus A**) and click the **Pick Operand B** button. In the Front viewport, select the frame. Make sure to right-click to turn off the Boolean command (see Figure 2-30). Select the glass and, using the MODIFY panel, change the height to **1/2"**. In the Front viewport, with the constrain to **Y** axis on, move the glass so that it is even with the top of the frame.

The strategy for drawing the legs is to create one complete leg and then use the array command to copy and rotate the legs into position. Begin by creating a cylinder in the Top viewport, using the previously covered methods (including the glass and the frame). Copy the settings for the cylinder from Figure 2-31 and name the object **legtop**. Make sure the constrain to **Y** button is on and in the Front viewport. Hold down the shift key and drag the cylinder upward to copy a total of four cylinders for all parts of the legs. From "legtop" part down, name the next cylinder **topmetal** and change its height to **1"**; the next cylinder should be called **centermetal** with a height of **4"** and a radius of **1/2"**. The next cylinder should be called **bottommetal** with a height of **1"**, and the last cylinder should be called **legbottom** with a height of **6"**. When the leg is complete, select the entire leg, and from the **GROUP** menu choose **group** (in a more complex situation, you might want to give each group a unique

| Parameters |  |
| --- | --- |
| Radius: | 0'1" |
| Height: | 0'4" |
| Height Segments: | 1 |
| Cap Segments: | 1 |
| Sides: | 50 |
| ☑ Smooth |  |
| ☐ Slice On |  |
| Slice From: | 0.0 |
| Slice To: | 0.0 |
| ☐ Generate Mapping Coords. |  |

▶ **Figure 2-31**

Settings for the *legtop*

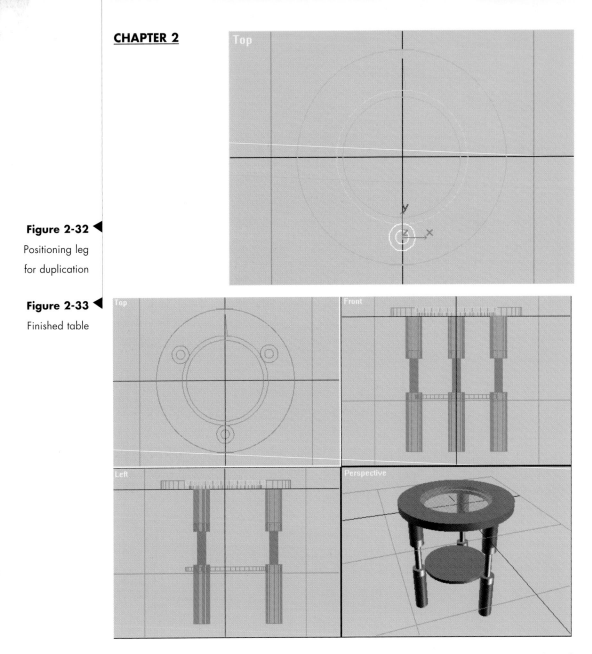

name). Position the leg group so that it is even with the bottom of the table. One edge of the leg should be touching the edge of the glass (see Figure 2-32). With the leg group selected, choose the **Use Transform Coordinate Center** button on the top menu bar. From the **Edit** menu choose **array**, and change the **Z Rotation** to **120** and the **Total in Array** to **3**. Then click on **OK**.

For the final step, select the glass and make a copy which should be named **centersupport**. Move the "*centersupport*" object between the "*bottommetal*" objects. When the table is finished, it should look something like the table in Figure 2-33 with the exception of the table colors (you can choose any colors).

## Using AutoCAD to Model the Table in a 3D Space

In the second method, the table is modeled directly into 3D modeling space, using 3D entities or geometric primitives and extruded lines and forms.

### AutoCAD Drawings and File Transfer

Before we begin to model the table, it is best to learn a little about working in the AutoCAD environment and about the special needs for transferring files between programs. In order for a drawing to transfer into 3DS MAX or other rendering program, all of the pieces should be solids, meshes, or primitives. In this case, the solid model is the easiest type on which to create the entire volume of the table. With the solid model, basic shapes can be created and then modified. Circles can be created and then extruded to a certain height (become a solid) or turned into a solid by revolving them around an axis. Once the model is created, these shapes can be edited, such as subtracting one from another or combining solid forms.

Certain things must be done in the AutoCAD drawing to ensure proper transfer to 3DS MAX. First, there must be a way for 3DS MAX to distinguish between parts of a drawing in order to edit and assign different materials to each piece. 3DS MAX works on objects, and the easiest way to identify objects in a drawing is by controlling the layer on which they are drawn. For example, if a table was modeled in AutoCAD, the glass top must be on a different layer than the wooden sections of the legs. In this way, 3DS MAX will treat the glass top as a separate object. It is easier to create a new layer and make it the current drawing layer before a piece is drawn. To distinguish the layers in the drawing, it is common to set each layer to a distinct color. This also helps you keep track of the pieces of a complex drawing. Give the layers names that make sense to you since the names will become the object names in 3DS MAX.

### User Coordinate System

The world and the current plan views will make more sense once you understand AutoCAD's user coordinate system (UCS). The **UCS** is the system in which you can define the origin and create a new plan to draw. The UCS setting determines the placement of the location of the origin (0,0,0) and the orientation of the XY plane and the Z axis. The default, or world coordinate system **(WCS)**, is the X axis as the horizontal screen dimension and the Y axis as a vertical to the screen dimension. The Z axis is perpendicular to the XY plane or is imagined

▶**TIP**

*The 3DS R4 and 3D Max share many concepts in file transfers.*

as coming out toward you from the computer screen. When you are working in the WCS, the XY plane can be navigated with the mouse; but to modify the location on the Z axis, the elevation must be altered. The elevation is set at <0'0"> at the start of the drawing. Objects will be set at the elevation that is current when they are created. Another way to work on the Z axis is to modify the thickness of an object. The thickness is also set to <0'0"> at the start of a drawing, but when it is set to another distance, an object will be drawn extruded along the Z axis to the thickness specified. To modify the thickness at the elevation of objects, at the command prompt, type **elev**. The prompt 'New Current Elevation <current>'will appear, displaying that to which it is currently set. You can type in the distance above 0 on the Z axis where you would like items to be drawn. After you hit [Enter], the prompt will read 'New Current Thickness <current>' with the current thickness displayed. You can either type in a new thickness or hit [Enter] to keep it the same.

There are a number of ways to change the UCS, or current drawing plane. The X, Y, and Z axes can be rotated a certain number of degrees; the UCS can be set to a current object. The UCS can be set by choosing three points, to name just a few. Make note of the UCS arrows. When the current UCS is different from the viewing angle, a broken pencil will be displayed to indicate that the view is not the plan where you can draw anything.

Working in 3D space may seem confusing at this point, but once you understand a few basics, it becomes easy to navigate. If you are confused about coordinates and UCS and axes and planes, here are a few hints to help you understand the meaning. Look around the room (the 3D environment) that you are in. Pick a corner of the room, and if you need to, go stand in it. Think of the floor as the computer screen. In the corner, you are at the origin of the screen, or the point (0,0,0). The X, Y, and Z axes are all 0 at the origin. The floor is the world drawing plane. When you look straight along one wall, in front of you is the Y axis, or the vertical direction of the computer screen. To the right of you is the X axis, or the horizontal direction of the computer screen. You and the walls rising behind you are extending into the Z axis - the axis that allows for volume of space (three-dimensionality). If you move 1' directly right and 2' directly forward, the bottoms of your feet are at the point (1',2',0'): 1' over on the X axis and 2' on the Y axis. Since your feet are touching the ground, you are at 0' on the Z axis. When viewing the world drawing plan (the plan view in the room), you would see the floor of the room, and basically all that is seen of you is the top of your head and shoulders. Look at everything in the room, and imagine how the objects would appear in the plan view. Think about their elevation (place on Z axis), where they would be drawn, and the thickness (span on Z axis) they would take up. Then imagine your computer screen as the 3D space. The better you become at visualizing your computer as a 3D space, the easier 3D modeling will be.

## Construct the Table

In general, before you start to model a 3D object, there are some preparation steps for successful 3D modeling with AutoCAD. First, make sure that you have a 3D representation of what you are working on. The representation can be a rough sketch or a detailed dimensional drawing. The representation will help with visualization, giving you a "place to start." Second, analyze the object, pulling apart the separate pieces that make up the object. Imagine or draw the object into simple geometric primitives that can be easily formed in the program. Finally, make a plan for modeling. The plan is personal, and often your plan of attack will not be the same even if the outcome is similar. The plan of attack is an outline of where to start and in what order the object will be formed. Your modeling skills will be refined as you develop your plan. It is common to start with the general and move to the smaller, specific details of an object. Another tactic is to start at the lowest point of an object and work your way up. Draw a room, beginning with the walls and floor to set the scale and boundaries of the drawing. With a smaller object such as this table, start with the glass tabletop to set the scale and space of the drawing by choosing the dominant element.

Begin by analyzing the table to find how the separate pieces comprise the object. Then construct them. The tabletop is made of a glass centerpiece with a wooden frame surrounding it and a ledge supporting the glass top. The wooden frame is one piece, so we can use the solid modeling methods plus the subtract feature to create the frame. The table legs are made from two materials. The easiest way to construct the legs is as a series of cylinders:

one cylinder for the bottom, three cylinders constructing the middle leg portion, and one cylinder for the top piece. The lower center circle is also a cylindrical construction. You may need to look at Figure 2-11 for reference.

To model the table, we will set up the layers before we begin. As you gain more experience modeling, you might start to construct new layers as you proceed. As was discussed earlier, the layers establish how the pieces will be distinguished from one another in 3D Studio. Even though there are only three materials making up this table, you need to construct more than three layers if there is a possibility of further editing in 3DS MAX.

Begin by setting up your drawing environment.
At the command prompt, type **Mvsetup** [Return].
To enable paper space, type **no** [Return].
To select architectural, type **A** (for architectural) [Return].
To select 3"=1', type **4** [Return].
To set the width of the paper, type **11** [Return].
To set the height of the paper, type **8.5** [Return].

A rectangular box will appear on your screen. To make sure the drawing environment is large enough to accommodate your drawing, move the cursor up to the right corner of your paper. Look at the bottom left corner of your screen. This is the coordinator display, and it shows you the maximum space for drawing your object. You can see with this setting that the area is too small for this project (only 2'8", 2'0"). To change the drawing environment, type **Mvsetup** to repeat the setup for the drawing environment, but this time select a smaller scale to increase the drawing space. Select **12** for a scale of 1"=1'. Keep the paper space set at 11" for the width and 8.5" for the height. Using **erase**, erase the small rectangle which is the previous paper setting. Now the paper is large enough to draw this table (10'10", 8' 2").

Set up a grid by typing **Grid** set at **2"** and set snap by typing **Snap** and set at **2"**.

**TIP** ◀

*In this exercise, every element of this table can be drawn from the plan view without changing UCS. All elements can be drawn by changing elevation.*

Start by setting up new layers for each element, and give each one a different color. To make a new layer, choose the following: **DATA\Layers**. A Layers menu will appear with the layer names and information about each layer. Type the layer name in the box near the bottom of the screen, then click on the **New** button. The layer name will then appear in the list of layers. Layers can be turned off and on for editing and viewing sections of the drawing by clicking on the **on\off** buttons when a layer is lit. Your layers should be **frame, glass, legb, legt, legcenter, leg-metal**, and **centersprt** (Figure 2-34). It is helpful to give each layer a distinct color. To set the color, click on the layer name to highlight the line, and then click on the **Set Color** button. Choose a color from the color menu that appears. Choose any colors you wish. Do this for each layer. Now highlight the Frame layer and click on the **Current** button to make this layer the current drawing layer; then click on **OK** to exit the layer control panel.

To start drawing the table frame, go to **TOOLS\Toolbars\Solids** from the pull-down menu to get the solids toolbar. Before you draw the cylinder, set the elevation to 20″ and do not change the thickness. To do this, type **elev**, [Return], **20″**, [Return], [Return]. Using the solids toolbar, select the **Cylinders-Center** option. Click on near the center point on the

▶ **TIP**

*The colors chosen for layers are arbitrary, but you may find it helpful to devise an individual system. For example, you may decide that all the elements of a table leg will be a shade of blue, the sections of the table-top frame will be a shade of red, and the glass will be a shade of yellow. This will help to group the objects visually and to distinguish certain sections from one another on the computer screen, helping to keep something clean and clear that could be visually messy.*

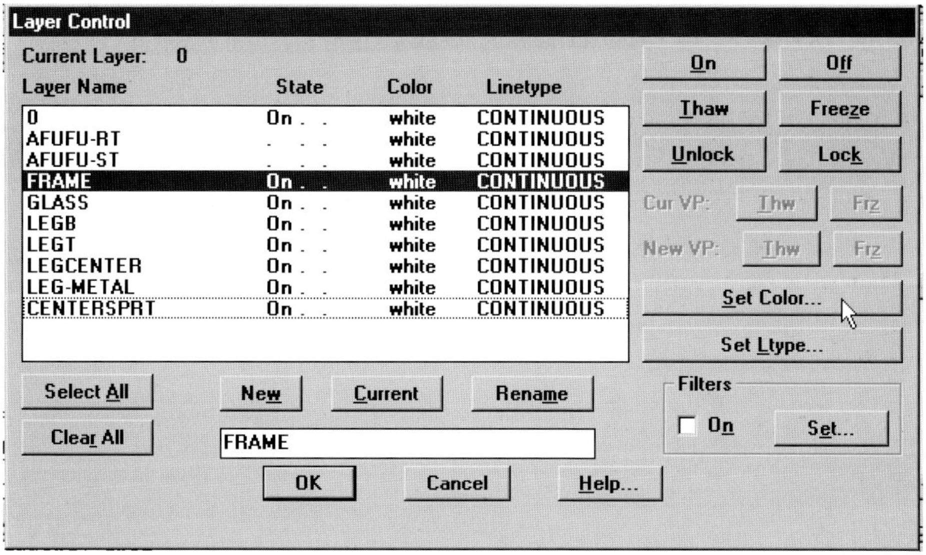

**Layer Control**

| Layer Name | State | Color | Linetype |
|---|---|---|---|
| Current Layer: 0 | | | |
| 0 | On . . | white | CONTINUOUS |
| AFUFU-RT | . . . | white | CONTINUOUS |
| AFUFU-ST | . . . | white | CONTINUOUS |
| FRAME | On . . | white | CONTINUOUS |
| GLASS | On . . | white | CONTINUOUS |
| LEGB | On . . | white | CONTINUOUS |
| LEGT | On . . | white | CONTINUOUS |
| LEGCENTER | On . . | white | CONTINUOUS |
| LEG-METAL | On . . | white | CONTINUOUS |
| CENTERSPRT | On . . | white | CONTINUOUS |

On · Off · Thaw · Freeze · Unlock · Lock · Cur VP: Thw Frz · New VP: Thw Frz · Set Color... · Set Ltype...

Select All · New · Current · Rename · Filters · On · Set... · Clear All · FRAME · OK · Cancel · Help...

▶ **Figure 2-34**

Setting up layers in AutoCAD

screen to set the center point. Set the radius at **1'4"** and set the height at **1"**. Draw another circle at the same center with a radius of **9"** and height of **1"**. This second circle is the center hole for the frame.

Then change the elevation to **20.5"** and **0"** for thickness to draw the ledge. Using the same circle center, draw a circle with a radius of **10"** and height at **0.5"**. Then from Modify Toolbar, select the **Subtract** command (found under the Explode icon) or type **Subtract**. Select the largest circle, and then [Return]. Then select the other two circles, and then [Return]. To see if this worked, go to view the 3D viewpoint. You may need to zoom in to view the object and then type **Hide** (Figure 2-35). To return to the drawing, type **Plan**, and then [Return] twice. To draw the glass, change the layer **glass** to the current layer. Keep the elevation at 20.5". Draw another cylinder from the same center point with a radius of **10"** and a height of **0.5"**.

To draw the legs, draw one complete leg, and then copy it for the other two. Begin changing the layer **legb** to the current layer. To draw the bottom part of the legs, change the elevation to **0"** and the thickness to **0"**. Draw a cylinder at the top portion of the circle (glass frame) with a radius of **2"** and a height of **8"**.

**Figure 2-35** ◀

Finished table-top

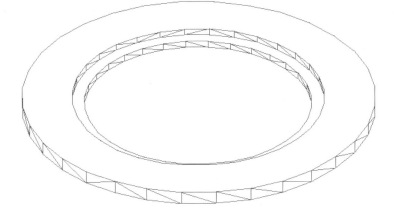

Now change the **layer leg-metal** to the current layer. Change the elevation to **8"** (which is on top of the bottom part of the leg). Leave the thickness at **0"**. Using the same center and the bottom part of the leg, draw a cylinder with a radius of **2"** and height of **1"**. Change the elevation to **13"**, and the thickness to **0"**. Draw the other metal piece by drawing a cylinder with a radius of **2"** and a height of **1"** (the same radius and height as in the previous one).

Now change the layer **legcenter** to the current layer. Change the elevation to **9"** thickness to **0"**. Using the same leg center, draw a cylinder with a radius of **0.5"** and height of **4"**. Now change the layer **legt** to the current layer. Change the elevation to **14"** and the thickness to **0"**. Using the same center of the leg, draw a cylinder with a radius of **2"** and height of **6"**.

Now look at the table using **VIEW\3D Viewpoints** (Figure 2-36). Copy this complete leg for the other two legs. To divide the circle into three parts to have equal distances between legs, draw a reference line through the center of the leg. Then type **Array**. Select the reference line. Use the **Polar** option. Then pick the table center as the center point of the array. Type **three** for the number of items. Angle to fill in 360 degrees, then hit [Enter]. Then click on **Yes** to rotate objects as they are copied. You now have the other two reference lines for the other legs.

Turn your snap **off.** Now copy the completed leg by typing **Copy**, then type **C** for "Crossing Sections" to make sure all parts of the leg are included, and select the leg. Then, using the center of the leg as the base point, copy the leg to both array points at the center of the array line. You can zoom in on the new legs and use the Move command to move the leg to a more accurate place (Figure 2-37).

▶ **Figure 2-36**
Finished table leg using method 2

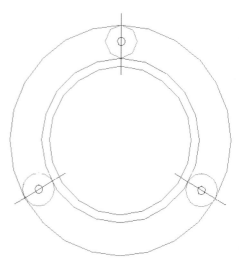

▶ **Figure 2-37**
Using polar array to position legs

**Figure 2-38** ◀
Finished table
using method 2

Now erase the vertical array guidelines. Choose **centersprt** to become the current layer in order to draw the center support circle with an elevation of **8″**, radius of **10″**, and **1″** for the height. The edge of the circle should touch all the legs.

It is also a good idea to make sure that you did not draw anything on the wrong layer before making the transfer to 3D Studio, since the change is much easier to make at this time. If you need to make a change, refer to the section above on changing the layer of an object. Now look at the table, using **VIEW\3D viewpoints**. Use **Hide** to view it as a solid; the image should look similar to Figure 2-38.

Once you are satisfied with the table, transfer the file. The file can be transferred directly by making a 3DS file in AutoCAD or by exporting the file by saving the drawing as a DXF file. Either one of the files can now be opened in 3D Studio for further study.

## Modeling a Complex 3D Environment in 3D Space

Three-dimensional modeling gets more complicated when we move to the modeling of environments (as opposed to objects). There are some basics to modeling the 3D environment that can make the task easier. When modeling a 3D object, we said that you should have a 3D representation. Pull apart the individual pieces, and then make a plan of attack for completing the piece. With larger spaces and complex objects not only is it difficult to get a complete 3D representation, but also if you tried to pull apart each individual piece and element before you began, it would be impossible to keep everything straight. To deal with this problem, the analysis and plan of attack require various levels of hierarchy that become important at different stages in the modeling process. Again, we are faced with the question, Where do I begin? The answer is to start with the general and work to the specific. Most often the exterior walls or the floor. If you are starting with the floor, you can deal with the individual sections of the floor and forget about the other pieces for the time being.

*This tutorial is based on Ms. Veronica Schroeder's senior studio project.*

Whichever is left is the next to be added. Once the exterior walls and floor are drawn in, the location for other elements is established in reference to these boundaries.

The creative application that we will be "walking through" is the modeling of a restaurant project. We do not go through every detail of 3D modeling as we did for the table; so if you are unfamiliar with the process, it is a good idea to review the table section (using method 2) or go through some references that came with your modeling program.

### Plan for Implementation

Although we are working directly in a 3D modeling space in the AutoCAD environment, most of the elements in the restaurant will be modeled as extruded polylines and other solid geometric primitives.

### Drawing setup

The drawing is set up in the same way as the table drawing, but the drawing limits must be different in order to fit the entire drawing into the drawing space. Choose Architectural Units, and select appropriate scale and paper size to accommodate your building; then set the Grid and Snap to easily start drawing the whole building.

### Stage 1: Floor

The restaurant building is basically a large rectangular space broken up into distinct areas by interior walls. In this case it seems logical to begin by drawing in the floor. Be sure to make separate layers for all the different elements in the drawing.

The restaurant is located on the third floor of an existing building. The amount of detail added to the first and second floors depends upon how the model will be used. Since the building will be part of an animation during the future study, only the staircases, one of the paths to the restaurant, and the restaurant itself will be modeled. The rest of the lower floors will not be added to the drawing. At this time it is more appropriate to change the elevation than to draw the restaurant level floor.

▶ **TIP**

*Even though the stages are separate, do not completely ignore all other elements or you might make mistakes. It is a good idea when planning a stage to ask yourself, How will what I am doing now be affected by interactions with elements in other stages, and does that change anything about my procedure?*

▶ **TIP**

*Always change the Grid and Snap to accommodate different drawing elements in your design. With a more complex space, it is easier to create the layers as you need them because it is next to impossible at this point to know what you will need.*

### Stage 2: Exterior walls

Once the floor is in place, the exterior walls can be built, using the floor as the guideline.

If the exterior of your building is quite complex or there is much exterior detailing, then the addition to the model can be very time-consuming and complicated. The amount of detail added to the building is a personal choice which is based on the needs of the model. Create a layer for exterior walls, and then draw a series of polylines that are the width and length of the four exterior walls (starting at elevation 0'0", which is ground level). Extrude the polylines to the height of the walls. After changing the UCS, add windows. The area for the window opening must be subtracted from the exterior wall form. A window frame and glass can then be created in the opening.

If you are planning on assigning a material to the inside of the exterior walls that is different from the material for the outside of the exterior walls, you must draw the walls as two pieces on separate layers, or 3D Studio will not recognize the distinct objects. It is easier to do this before you work with the window subtraction and addition. For the restaurant project, the exposed brick will remain in the interior, so this does not need to be done.

The subtraction of the windows is a bit complicated. One way to do this is to begin by drawing guidelines to mark the location of the windows, and then draw one box the size of the opening. Copy to the marked locations. Then the boxes are subtracted together. Changing the UCS is necessary for the copy and subtraction process.

**TIP ◄**

*To make things easier, use the Copy command whenever possible, for example, when drawing moldings for identical windows.*

Now that the openings are subtracted and the exterior walls are full of holes, it is time to build the windows and doors. Start by building one complete window; then construct the frame (polyline or solids box), subtract the center, and add the glass. Then copy the frame and glass together to the other window openings.

### Stage 3: Interior walls and interior wall detailing

It is now time to break up the interior space by building walls. You will also need to subtract any openings as you did with the exterior walls. Base, crown, and interior window moldings can also be added to the space.

Draw the polylines, or box the length and width of the interior walls. Extrude the polylines to the wall height. Add base and crown moldings. The moldings can be drawn from the world plan view by changing the elevations and extruding for the heights. The moldings can also be drawn by changing the UCS to an elevation view of a wall (Front\Right\Left\Back), drawing them as polylines or boxes, and then extruding for certain thicknesses (heights).

### Stage 4: Flooring and ceiling details

Even though the floor is already drawn in, much more needs to be done for the finished product. Begin by adding the connection between the floors and the staircase. Build the changes in the flooring level, and add another layer of flooring onto every floor space that will require a distinct material in later rendering (each on a separate layer). And finally, draw an object for every distinct section of the ceiling.

### Stage 5: Interior furnishings and details

The interior furnishings are fun to add to the space because the drawing will really begin to make sense. For the restaurant, you only need to draw one of each type of table and chair and then copy them to the other locations. The amount of detail added is again a personal choice. If any of the items included in the restaurant need custom building, more details might be necessary in the model.

All that is left is the remaining details and light fixtures. If you use AutoCAD, you may load the **RESTAUNT.DWG** from the CH2 subdirectory included on the CD attached to the back of the book. If you are using other CAD software, you can load **RESTAUNT.DXF** on the CD.

▶ **TIP**

*If the drawing is getting visually messy, making it difficult to understand the lines, then the layers that are not currently being modified can be turned off and turned back on when needed. Proceed through the addition of flooring and ceiling details, changing the elevation and UCS whenever necessary.*

▶ **TIP**

*Create every necessary layer for a table. Then model the tables, copying, modifying, and using any similar parts from the completed tables. Copy the tables to all the desired locations.*

## Summary

These tutorials introduced two practical methods for 3D modeling as well as several of the basic tools in 3D Studio and AutoCAD. By using the modeling techniques covered in these tutorials, it is possible to begin exploring the potential of 3D modeling in visualization applications. The better you understand the 3D modeling environment and the better you plan the modeling procedure, the more successful you will be. Changing the concept from using the computer as a 2D drafting tool to a 3D modeling or sculpting tool is the key to realizing the true potential of the computer in the design visualization field.

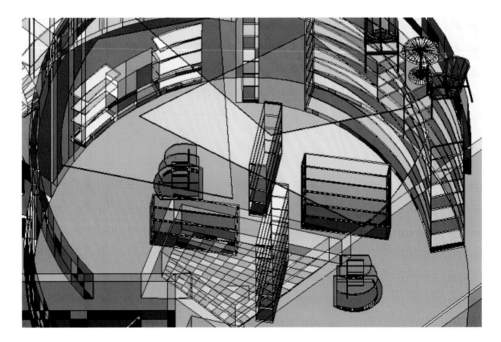

Bookstore with cappuccino bar, rendered axonometric                    **Ann McGovern**

*When we were children, all we needed to know about color was contained in a box of crayons. Our color spectrum consisted of 64 hues with memorable names and a sharpener on the back of the box. The digital designer is provided with a much larger color palette — some computer programs can define over 16 million hues.*

Colour (and this is something the colour-shy must try to grasp) is not a decorative part of architecture, but its organic medium of expression.

- Theo Van Doesburg

Chapter written by Professor Kathleen Gibson.

# Introduction

From the early experiments of Sir Isaac Newton, exploring whether color was present in light, through complex mathematical arrangements based on a hue's *X,Y,Z* location (as defined by the Commission Internationale de l'Eclairage in 1931), each discovery has contributed to our understanding of color. Theories and cultural beliefs about the meaning and use of color have been numerous and important determinants in the fields of interior design and architecture. In 1856 specific rules for color placement on three-dimensional objects were proposed by Owen Jones in his book *Grammar of Ornament*. Placement was linked to surface location: Blue was to be used on concave surfaces, yellow on convex, and red on underside surfaces. Several decades later it was the lack of color, not its placement, which became the ideology used to characterize the international style of architecture. However, many modern architects and designers still valued color as an important design element.

As early as 1910, Le Corbusier explained that the brilliance of white surfaces was noticeable only when contrasted with intense colors (Abercrombie, 1990). His artistic use of bold color is well documented in his architectural commissions. Contemporary designers have also recognized the value of color in the built environment. Emilio Ambasz (1980) reviews the work of Luis Barragan, which ". . . is based on a few constructive elements bound together by a mystical feeling, an austerity exhaulted by the glory of his brilliant colors." Like Barragan, every designer wants to develop a poetic color palette to enrich the architectural integrity of the interior space. It is this study of color relationships which lends itself to the computer and digital color.

Women's boutique, final rendering                                    **Haewon Shim**

# Concepts

## Seeing and Identifying Color

*The commercial printing industry uses colored inks which are unique to their printing process - primaries include cyan, yellow, and magenta. Many times black is combined with the primaries in what is called a four-color process.*

A powerful communicator of information and pleasure, color assists people in their everyday activities. Color is a sensation of light on the eye's retina. This visual sensation occurs when light is reflected into the eye from a surface, such as the skin of a ripe tomato. The eye immediately translates the information to the brain, which recognizes the redness of the tomato's skin.

Colors are identified by three dimensions: hue, value, and saturation. The term used to differentiate the red of a tomato from the red of a ruby is referred to as a color's **hue**. Variations of hues are created by mixing together different quantities of primary colors. Dyes, stains, and paint pigments are governed by **subtractive primaries** consisting of red, yellow, and blue. Secondary colors are a mixture of two subtractive primaries, commonly called orange, green, and violet. **Additive primaries** deal with light and are responsible for what is displayed on a computer monitor. Primary colors for digital graphics consist of red, green, and blue. Combining two digital primaries will produce secondary colors - mixing red and green will produce yellow; mixing red and blue will result in magenta; and combining green and blue will produce cyan (Figure 3-1).

**Figure 3-1** ◀
Subtractive and additive primaries and secondaries

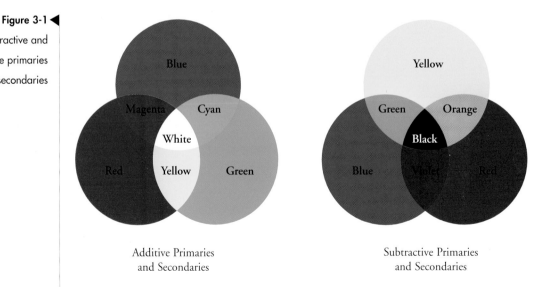

Additive Primaries
and Secondaries

Subtractive Primaries
and Secondaries

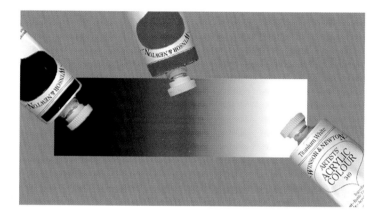

**Value** refers to the lightness or darkness of a color. For example, combining white and red pigments will produce a tint of red, commonly called pink (Figure 3-2). **Shades** of red appear at the opposite end of the value continuum and contain a mixture of black and red pigments. Producing shades and tints of a hue on the computer is similar to that of pigment. Features of graphic software enable the digital artist to vary the quantity of white light or black (the absence of light) to replicate hundreds of values for each imaginable hue. **Saturation**, also called **chroma**, measures the purity or intensity of a color. Neutralized colors - those with low intensity levels - are also referred to as **tones**. With traditional pigments, color tones are created by (1) mixing the color with gray or (2) mixing the color with its complement (the hue opposite the original on a standard color wheel). Thus, mixing red with its complement - green - or with gray pigment will result in a dusty or dull rose-colored tone (Figure 3-3). As with previous color dimensions, saturation is easily manipulated within graphic applications. The digital artist adds more or less of the hue's additive complement to vary a color's intensity (Figure 3-1).

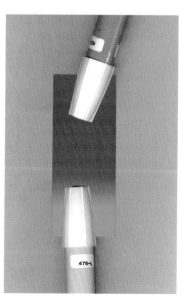

## Organizational Methods

For centuries, scientists and artists have tried to define and organize color using various charts and methods. In 1915, art teacher Albert Munsell developed a three-dimensional color system based on visual acuity to represent the three dimensions of color pigment. Each color variation is distinguished by its individual hue, value, and chroma and located on the model according to these three continuums. Although his was not the first 3D model, Munsell's color system has remained a popular system for color instruction and identification (De Grandis, 1986).

Scientists approached the subject of color from a different perspective. In 1872, physicist Sir James Maxwell created a mathematical rationale for the organization of color. He identified three primary components of light (red, green, blue) and charted them within each corner of a right-angle triangle. For the first time in history, secondary, tertiary, and quaternary hues could be calculated by finding their distance along the X and Y axes. Fifty years later, the Commission Internationale de l'Eclairage (**CIE**) expanded on Maxwell's system by calculating color not only along the X and Y axes, but also along the Z dimension. This breakthrough enabled manufacturers to provide greater color reliability and accuracy for their products. Updated in 1976, the CIE Uniform Space system has become the industry standard for color identification and specification throughout the world (Norman, 1990). Both systems are valuable for the digital artist. Software packages and computer monitors define color mathematically; digital artists understand color visually.

# Cognition

## Color Displays

Graphic software applications control color through the use of **color gamuts**. Tristimulus gamuts use three channels of information to mix and define color. The most common color gamut is **RGB** (red, green, blue). Custom colors are created by changing the overall quantity of the additive primaries: red, green, and blue. Removing blue from the mixture results in yellow; removing red produces cyan; and removing green creates magenta. Adding full strengths of all three primaries produces white light; removal of all primaries results in black. Another popular tristimulus color gamut is **HLS** (hue, luminance, saturation). Color customization through the HLS gamut occurs by manipulating an individual color's hue, value, and saturation levels. A four-variable color gamut requires four channels of information to define a color. **CYMK** (cyan, yellow, magenta, black) is the most common of the four-variable gamuts. Although mixing all three primaries (CYM) should theoretically result in black, it is not a pure black. Thus, the decision to add black ink to the three primary inks creates a better-quality printed image. Choosing the appropriate color gamut depends on the type of final output desired by the digital artist. Images to be projected from the computer screen should specify an RGB color gamut, whereas images which will be printed should choose a CYMK color gamut to ensure color accuracy.

## Color Quality

Digital images produced with paint programs are typically **raster-based** and consist of small squares of color called **pixels**. Some raster images may appear to have rough color boundaries while others have smooth transitions between areas of color (Figure 3-4). The key factor in raster image quality is resolution. **Image resolution** controls the spacing of pixels within an image. As the number of **pixels per inch** (ppi) increases, the level of image clarity and detail also increases. Simple graphic applications have a set image resolution, while more sophisticated programs enable the user to specify image resolution quality. **Bit resolution**

▶ Figure 3-4

Contrast of image resolution

(more commonly called **pixel depth**) is the quantity of color information stored in each pixel. Simple software applications create images with **4-bit** color and are limited to 16 colors or gray values. Mid-level paint programs use **8-bit** color and have 256-color capability. Sophisticated graphic programs use either **16-bit** or **24-bit** color depth and can provide the digital artist with up to 16 million hues. As image and bit resolutions increase, the file size of a digital image grows proportionally. For example, an image at 200 ppi is 4 times the file size of the same image at 100 ppi. Effectively balancing image quality and file size is important for the digital artist.

Computers produce color images via different types of peripheral devices; the most common are monitors, printers, film, and video and CD-Rom recorders. Again, resolution is an important variable for producing quality color output. Monitors display digital color by dividing the screen into narrow vertical stripes, alternating red, green, and blue phosphor (light). These narrow stripes, called the **dot pitch**, refer to the monitor's resolution. Higher dot-pitch values create better image resolution. An acceptable dot-pitch resolution for a desktop computer monitor is 0.28 millimeter (mm). Similar to the commercial printing industry, computer **printers** use a four-color process. Inks of cyan, yellow, magenta, and black are used to produce full-color printed images. Printer resolution is measured in **dots per inch** (dpi). Recent advances in color technology have made 300-dpi printers very affordable for the digital artist. Better-quality, photograph-like images require color printer resolutions of 600 dpi or higher. Finally, digital images can be transferred to film via two methods. **Component color** is the highest quality because transmittance of RGB information occurs on three separate channels or wires. Videotape formats that support component color are Hi8 and Betacam. The second method of image transfer is **composite color**, which converts color data into one channel. While simplifying the process, this method also reduces image quality. VHS, NTSC, PAL, and SECAM television formats all use composite color.

To ensure color image consistency, peripheral devices must be adjusted to match a standard color gamut. **Color calibration** is the process of comparing reference images and value charts provided by the hardware manufacturer to the monitor, scanner, printer, and film recorder. Even with calibration, color accuracy with printers is difficult to achieve. Variations occur due to paper quality, ink consistency, and humidity.

## Color Creation and Manipulation

Color is rarely seen in isolation. It continually changes due to environmental, psychological, and physical factors. Color perception is also affected by the chromatic relationship and arrangement of pigments. In his book *Color Drawing*, Michael Doyle (1981) demonstrates the layering of markers and colored pencils together to achieve a desired hue. First, a foundation of pale burgundy is applied using a marker. Doyle then uses an orange pencil and later a canary yellow pencil to layer color over the marker base; a new, hybrid color materializes. This method of layering color is common with traditional media. A second method used with traditional media is the mixing of paint or powdered dyes to create new hues. Creating color by using digital tools has similarities to both of these traditional methods.

Unlike with traditional media, the digital artist has broader control over color variables. Elements may include, but are not limited to, hue, value, saturation, pattern, texture, opacity, transparency, illuminance, and reflectance. Hue, value, and saturation controls are common with most digital paint programs, whereas some of the more complex options are only available with more sophisticated graphic applications. Mixing electronic color involves adjusting the RGB, HLS, or CYMK gamut controls provided within individual software packages (Figure 3-5). Digital color manipulation can be more interactive than with traditional media due to factors of time and permanence. Instead of waiting for markers or acrylic paint to dry before each hue can be evaluated, the artist has new digital colors immediately available for use. Digital color manipulation, application, and deletion can be easily accomplished without retaining unwanted residue, as happens with traditional color media. Both benefits enable color experimentation without penalty of unreversable decisions.

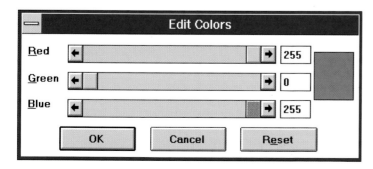

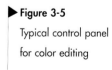
▶ **Figure 3-5**

Typical control panel for color editing

Defining digital color through the method of layering requires adjustment of the **opacity** and **transparency** qualities of the color palette. For example, layering a transparent circle of yellow over an area of red will produce an orange hue at the intersection of the two original colors. The amount of transparency for each hue is controlled by the digital artist through a sliding numeric scale ranging from 0 (transparent) to 100 (opaque). Adjustments in opacity and transparency values appear immediately on the screen, making this a truly interactive experience for the digital artist. Color creation parallels have been drawn between traditional and digital methods; however, specialized digital painting features provide new tools for color application. Graphic software enables the digital artist to define patterned brushes, specify rendering styles, and experiment with different paper textures. Each of these features enables images to be created which have a less static, computerized appearance, simulating everything from a manual watercolor painting to a pen and ink drawing (Figure 3-6).

▶ **Figure 3-6**

Computer-generated
pen-and-ink rendering

# Applications

## Textile Design with Photoshop 4.0

**Figure 3-7** ◀
Tutorial: final image
of textile fabric

The following hands-on tutorial will give you experience in creating and manipulating the color scheme of a custom textile pattern (Figure 3-7). This tutorial has been written using Adobe Photoshop (1996), but the same idea could be accomplished using simpler paint programs such as Paint or CorelDraw. Photoshop may also be used for other design-related tasks: to add a color base to floor plans and perspectives (Figure 3-8) or to achieve a final presentation rendering (Figure 3-9).

Begin by initializing the Photoshop program. Load the file called **TEXTILE.PSD.** This file contains a 2D drawing of a textile pattern, originally created with AutoCAD software. To load the file, use the command **FILE\Open** located at the top left of the screen. You will find the file located within the CH3 subdirectory on the enclosed CD. Once it is located, click on the filename and accept all other defaults by clicking on **OK**. A black-and-white drawing of a textile pattern should appear on your screen (Figure 3-10).

**Figure 3-8** ◀
Adding limited flat
color to a scanned
perspective drawing

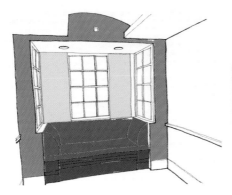

**Figure 3-9** ◀
Full-color rendering
of manual drawing
using digital
painting tools

Photoshop contains three command systems: pull-down menus along the top of the screen, a toolbox of icons along the left margin, and various roll-out palettes. Before continuing any further, familiarize yourself with the location of commands and icons which will be used in this tutorial (Figure 3-11).

| | |
|--|--|
| Marquee | |
| Magic Wand | |
| Paintbucket | |
| Eyedropper | |
| Zoom | |
| Eraser | |
| Pencil | |
| Foreground color | |
| Switch colors | |
| Background colors | |
| Default colors | |

▶ **Figure 3-10**
Tutorial: black-and-white drawing of textile pattern

▶ **Figure 3-11**
Photoshop commands needed for tutorial

▶ **TIP**
*Extended features of many commands are found by pressing the [Shift], [Control], or [Alt] keys in conjunction with a tool. Refer to the command prompt line at the bottom of the screen for additional instructions.*

The Marquee and Magic Wand are two of the most frequently used tools in Photoshop. Both are used to select a bounded area on the digital canvas. While the Marquee tool defines only rectangular areas, the Magic Wand selects any irregular area defined by similarly-colored pixels. The Marquee tool is also valuable for deselecting an area or shape.

The following steps will show you how to fill selected areas with color. Click on the Magic Wand tool with your mouse to activate the command. Use your mouse to click within the interior area of one of the ovals on the screen. Do not click on the shape's black boundary. A flashing, dashed line should now appear to designate an active selection set. If more than the oval was selected, use the EDIT\Undo command to deselect. Or another way to deselect an area is to activate the Marquee tool and then click on a point anywhere on the screen with your mouse. If you do not currently have an oval selected, repeat the above steps.

# CHAPTER 3

You are now ready to begin the second part of this process, which will fill the selected oval with color. Locate the Foreground\Background icon at the bottom of the toolbox. Use your mouse to click on the left foreground color box. The Color Picker palette appears. Note the RGB and HSB (hue, saturation, brightness) controls in the middle of the palette. To select the fill color, either you can choose (by clicking with the mouse) from the hues displayed in the large area to the left, or you can manipulate the gamut values to define custom hues (Figure 3-12). Select any color you wish to apply to the textile drawing and click on **OK**. Your color choice should now appear in the Foreground area on the toolbox. Now apply your selected color within the predefined oval. Click on the **Paintbucket** icon to activate the command. Center the mouse over the selected oval shape, and using the mouse, click once within the interior of the oval. The oval automatically fills with the designated color. Deselect the selection area by accessing the Marquee tool and clicking anywhere within the textile drawing. Repeat this sequence of commands to fill in other shapes with different colors. Save your work by using the **FILE\Save** command.

**Figure 3-12** ◀
Color Picker
dialogue box in
Photoshop

To get a closer look at your work, use the **Zoom** tool (magnification glass). First click on the icon to activate the command, and then click anywhere on the drawing. The drawing should appear closer (larger) to you. To reverse this process, hold down the [Alt] key (located at the lower left of the keyboard) while clicking on the drawing. Your drawing should return to its original size. Note that a plus or a minus sign occurs within the icon to denote positive or negative zooming.

To capture a previous color from your textile drawing, try the **Eyedropper** tool. Click on the icon to activate the command. Using your mouse, click on top of the color you used to fill the first oval. The color should now appear in the Foreground area at the bottom of the toolbox.

Colors are easily changed by reselecting the same area and filling again with a second hue. There is no need to erase the first color prior to replacing it with another hue. Erasing will replace both fills and boundary lines with the Background color. The Background color is white by default (although yours may be different). To erase both the fill color and boundary lines, click on the **Eraser** icon to activate the command. Hold down the mouse and drag over the area you wish to erase. Use the **EDIT\Undo** command to restore the erased area.

To limit the area of erasure, first define a selection set, using the Magic Wand or Marquee tool, and then drag the eraser over the selected area. Now only pixels inside the selected area will be erased.

As already seen, the Paintbucket tool applies color in an even, consistent manner. However, sometimes a more random color application is desired. To accomplish this effect, try the **Paintbrush** tool. This command comes with many options. For example, use the **WINDOW\Show Brushes** command to display the Brushes palette (Figure 3-13). Features located on this palette enable the user to specify the size of the brush and the edge softness or hardness of the tool. Using the mouse, pick a medium-sized brush to make it current (denoted by a heavy black border). Return to the textile drawing. Hold down on the mouse button and drag in a stroking manner to apply color in one of the shapes on the drawing. Note that controlling the paintbrush via the mouse takes some practice. You may choose to use the **EDIT\Undo** command at this time to remove any haphazard paint strokes. To control painting within the lines, (1) use the Magic Wand tool to first select a shape's interior; (2) activate the Paintbrush tool; and (3) make broad strokes with the mouse. Note that color appears only within the selected area. If you like what you've done so far, this is a good time to **FILE\Save** your work.

▶ **TIP**

*Using the Eyedropper tool ensures an accurate match to existing hues. This tool is especially helpful when you are trying to match colors contained within an imported photograph or scanned image.*

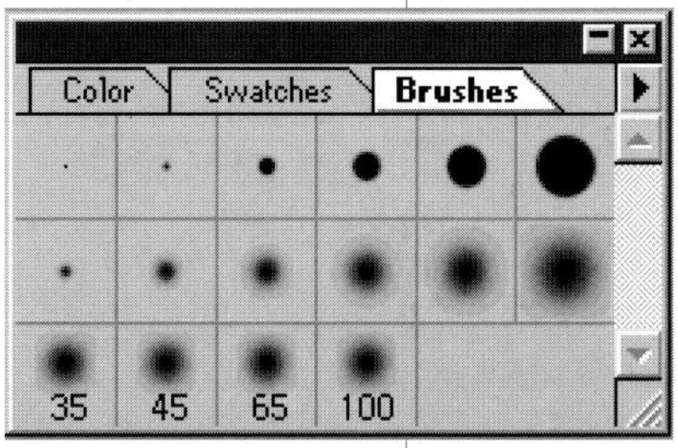

▶ **Figure 3-13**

Brushes palette in Photoshop

▶ **TIP**

*To undo your last action, use the EDIT\Undo command. Note that Undo is not cumulative; it only works for the last action.*

**TIP** ◀

*To create straight lines with the Pencil tool, hold down the [Shift] key while drawing. Another method for drawing straight lines is to use the Line tool. Special features found in the Line Options folder (double-click on the icon) enable you to set line widths and specify lines with arrowheads.*

Use the **Pencil** tool to add some free-form lines to the existing textile pattern. The marks you are about to draw will use the Foreground color. Pencil marks are created by clicking on a starting point with the mouse, holding down the mouse button, dragging, and releasing to finish the command. As with most of the toolbox commands, the options folder enables changes to the opacity and various other characteristics of each individual tool. Access the Pencil Options folder by double-clicking on the Pencil icon. Use the mouse to increase the transparency value by dragging to the left the small triangle located under 100 percent opacity. Draw another line and compare the difference to full opacity. Continue to experiment with the transparency feature. Close the Pencil Options folder by clicking on the **X** in the upper right corner of the folder.

The **EDIT\Cut** command enables the user to remove a predefined selection set. Note that cutting away a nonfloating selection set will automatically replace the original area with the Background color. To see how this works, change the Background color to anything but white. Next, define the selection set by using either the Marquee or Magic Wand. Activate the **EDIT\Cut** command; the selection set will be removed and in its place, the Background color will appear.

This tutorial has only scratched the surface of Photoshop's features. Additional information is contained in the following tutorial and in the software manuals provided by Adobe Photoshop.

## Portfolio Page Using Photoshop 4.0

This tutorial will build upon the knowledge already gained from the previous exercise. Using Photoshop, you will produce a visual portfolio page consisting of several imported images and text (Figure 3-14). Another avenue to explore on your own with Photoshop is the creation of surface materials for use in the digital libraries of 3D rendering applications (see Chapter 4). Again, this tutorial will focus only on commands pertinent to the portfolio exercise. At completion, you should have a useful working knowledge of Photoshop; however, additional study (through software manuals and other means) is recommended to increase knowledge and proficiency.

Before proceeding, familiarize yourself with the location of commands and icons which will be used in this tutorial (Figure 3-15).

If you are not already in Photoshop, initialize the program. Begin by creating a new file using the command **FILE\New**. A dialogue box will appear. Type in the filename **Page** in the designated box. Write down the current image (file) size. Change the **Width** to 8″ and the **Height** to 10″. Compare the image size now; it should be much larger. Finally, change the resolution to 150 pixels/inch. The default is set for the standard monitor resolution. Higher resolutions are recommended for quality printing. Compare the image size one last time. Each factor was responsible for increasing the image file size. Accept all other defaults in the dialogue box.

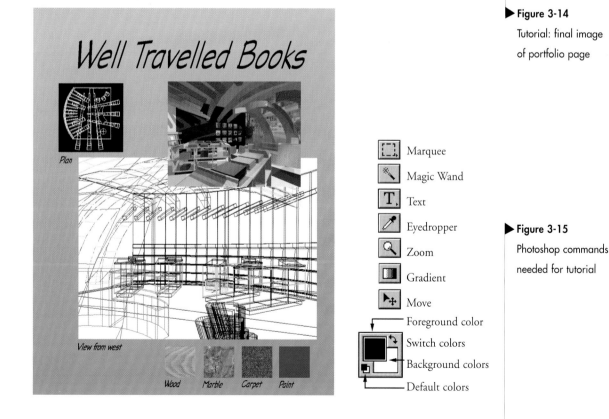

▶ **Figure 3-14**

Tutorial: final image of portfolio page

▶ **Figure 3-15**

Photoshop commands needed for tutorial

**TIP ◀**

*Keep in mind that very large image files may exceed the amount of memory in the print buffer, resulting in printing problems. If during this exercise you receive an error, stating that the Scratch Disk is full, then (1) reduce the overall size of the image to 4" by 6", (2) simplify your project by deleting some images, or (3) provide more space on your hard drive.*

A blank page should now appear on your screen. If rulers do not appear on the top and left margins, use the **VIEW\Show Rulers** command.

Begin this exercise by creating a background of gradating color. Define the Foreground color as beige and the Background color blue. Click on the **Gradient** tool to initialize the command. To define the direction of color gradation, click on a beginning point at the top of the page, hold and drag the mouse to the bottom of the page, and release it to define the ending point. A soft gradation between the foreground and background colors will now appear on the portfolio page.

### Importing Images

Next, learn how to import and crop a scanned image onto your portfolio page. In past versions of Photoshop you had to create individual layers. With Photoshop 4.0, layers are created automatically every time you create or import something new on the canvas. **FILE\Open** the file **FLOORPLN.TIF** found in the CH3 subdirectory on the enclosed CD. A new image will appear on the screen. Because this image was the last to be accessed, it is the current image. Your portfolio page may have neutralized the color of its title bar and image because it is no longer the current image file. To make your portfolio page current again, pick a spot anywhere on the canvas with the mouse, and the original title bar color will return. Another way to know which image file is current is to look at the Layers palette. The LAYERS palette will only display layers on the current image file. If not already displayed you can find the LAYERS palette under the WINDOW pull-down menu.

Make the **FLOORPLN.TIF** file current again by clicking it with your mouse. Using the Marquee tool, define a square tightly around just the floor plan. Once the selection set is defined, use the **IMAGE\Crop** command to delete much of the extraneous background around the plan. Next, use the **Move** tool to copy the image to the portfolio page. With the mouse, click on the floor plan image and hold; drag the image to the portfolio page and release. The portfolio file will now be current. Note that a new layer, called Layer 1, now appears in the Layers palette. Double-click on **Layer 1** to access a dialogue box with additional options. Rename the layer by typing *Plan*. You may choose to vary the layer's *transparency* by typing in a new opacity value in the dialogue box. Exit the dialogue box by clicking on **OK**. Select the floor plan image by using the **Move** tool, and reposition it to the upper left corner of the canvas. To remove the original **FLOORPLN.TIF** file from the screen, first make it current and then close it by clicking on the **X** in the title bar.

Use **EDIT\Open** to open another file called **WIRE.TGA**, located in the CH3 subdirectory. Repeat the above steps to place this image onto your portfolio page. Name this layer *Wire*. Verify that this layer is now current. While other layers may be repositioned to enhance the overall composition, the background layer must always remain at the bottom of the Layers palette (Figure 3-16). To reposition the Wire layer, click on the name of the layer with your mouse, hold, and drag below the *Plan* layer. Layers may even be deleted by dragging them into the Trash icon at the lower right corner of the Layers palette. The Eye icon, in the left column, indicates that the layer is visible. Click on the **Eye** icon to toggle off the layer, making it invisible to you. Only visible layers will print.

Repeat the above steps again to import the following files from the CD into your portfolio page: **PHOTO.TGA, WOOD.TIF,** and **MARBLE.TIF, CARPET.TIF**

▶ **NOTE**

*Layers is a powerful software feature that enables the digital artist to separate and manage elements on the canvas. It functions similarly to a cartoon cel, which is constructed from several sheets of layered acetate, each containing a portion of the animated scene. In Photoshop 4.0, layers are automatically created every time a new element is created.*

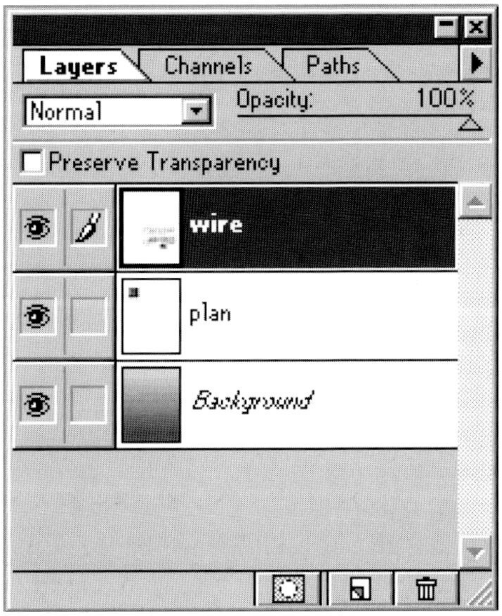

▶ **Figure 3-16**
Layers palette in Photoshop

**TIP** ◀

*If the number of layers is becoming cumbersome, you may choose to combine them into one background layer. Use the LAYER\Flatten Image command to accomplish this task.*

To create the paint chip, begin by creating a new layer. In the Layers palette, click on the black, triangular arrow located to the top right of the palette. From the options displayed, click on **New Layer** and name it **Paint**. Create a rectangle with the **Marquee** tool and fill it with color using the **Paintbucket** tool. Arrange all of the images into a final composition by using the **Move** tool. This is a good time to use **FILE\Save** to save your work.

You are finished importing images and now will add text to your portfolio page. Note that the text you are about to create will use the Foreground color as shown in the toolbox. If this color is not acceptable to you, define a new Foreground color (black) at this time. Select the **Text** tool from the toolbox. Although you expect something to happen, nothing will until you define a starting point on the canvas with your mouse. Click on a point under the floor plan image. A dialogue box will appear. Change the **Font Size** to **12 points**. Type in the word **Plan** and accept all other defaults. The text will now appear on your portfolio page on its own layer. To reposition the text, use the **Move** tool. Continue to add titles to the other imported images. Save your work by using the **FILE\Save** command.

## Manipulating Text and Images

**TIP** ◀

*If you receive an error (nothing in selection set) or have problems selecting text or an image, you need to be located within the correct layer. Click on the layer's name in the Layers palette that contains the item; the layer becomes current and is visibly highlighted. You may now select an item without a problem.*

The following series of commands can be used to easily manipulate bitmap images and text. All are located under the **LAYER\Transform** pull-down menus. Begin by selecting one word of text with the Marquee tool. Mirror the word horizontally or vertically using the **LAYER\Transform\Flip Horizontal** command. If you do not want the word to remain as it is, use the **EDIT\Undo** command at this time. Next, you will see how to rotate the word. Verify that the text is still selected. Initiate the **LAYER\Transform\Rotate** command and, using the mouse, drag the corner to rotate the text. Again, use **EDIT\Undo** to return the word to its original format. To enlarge or reduce the word's size, you will increase or decrease its scale. At this time verify that the word is still selected. Initiate the command **LAYER\Transform\Scale**. A thin border with four selection **handles** (small squares at corners) now appears around the word. Use your mouse to click on one handle, hold, drag, and then release the mouse. If you wish the word to remain proportional when scaling, hold down the [Shift] key while dragging. Accept the scaling effect by clicking the selection set with the mouse (represented by a hammer icon). The handles will disappear. Deselect the word using the Marquee tool.

The following three commands are similar in function to **Scale**. To further alter the word selection, experiment with the **Skew, Perspective,** and **Distort** commands (Figure 3-17).

The following set of commands is located under the FILTER pull-down menu. Filters change the current distribution of pixels, thereby producing a new, distorted effect. Begin by using the **Marquee** tool to select the photo image. Note that most of the following commands give you a preview of the effect and prompt you to accept or reject the proposed change.

Initiate the following command sequence: **FILTER\Noise\Add Noise**. A dialogue box will appear. Experiment with the amount slider bar and review changes; accept when you are satisfied. Freely experiment with the other filters, especially **Artistic** and **Sketch**, before completing the tutorial (Figure 3-18).

▶ **TIP**

*It is always better to create text at the appropriate point size than to scale afterward; scaling distorts the pixels and creates a blurry image.*

# Normal Text

## Perspective

### Skew

### Distort

▶ **Figure 3-17**
Resulting text after skew, perspective, and distort commands

▶ **Figure 3-18**
Artistic distortion using Photoshop filters option

## Summary

Color surrounds our everyday life. Along with materiality, color is the most intimate and personal of design elements. It has the power to stimulate activity, symbolize cultural values, and communicate information about ourselves and others. However, color is not a simple subject; it deserves thoughtful study. Computer graphics has the power to provide an untapped freedom for color study. Sixteen million opportunities, in addition to patterned bitmaps, will challenge designers to view color, pattern, and texture in a new light. The possibilities for creative minds are endless.

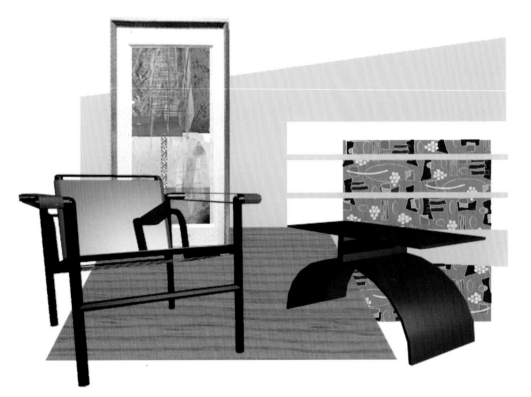

Corporate reception area, presentation of a board                    **Jeanne Mercer**

# RENDERING SURFACE MATERIALS AND TEXTURE

# 4

Materials are an important component in the creation of architecture and interior spaces. A project's palette of surface materials is communicated in two ways: initially through sketches and rendered illustrations, and later through the production of construction documents. Computer software is available to aid the designer in both modes of communication.

> ...materials are the gateway of our civilization as they affect every phase of our life.
> - George Beylerian

Chapter written by Professor Kathleen Gibson.

# Introduction

Throughout this century, a variety of theories about surface appearance have made an impact on the creative arts. In 1908 Viennese architect Adolf Loos defined surface decoration as a crime against the economy. In response to the highly decorative style of the Victorian period, Loos believed ornament to be a waste of money, material, and human labor. However, other contemporary architects and designers have not shunned surface decoration entirely. Louis Sullivan believed that a beautiful building can be devoid of any ornamentation; however, a "...decorated structure, harmoniously conceived, well considered, cannot be stripped of its system of ornament without destroying its individuality" (Malnar & Vodvarka, 1992, p. 268). Authors Malnar and Vodvarka (1992) conclude that ornament must be an initial design intent and that its expression must be inclusive with the form and surfaces it enhances. Likewise in 1932, Frank Lloyd Wright wrote that "expressive changes of surface, emphasis of line, especially textures of materials or imaginative pattern may go to make facts more eloquent, form more significant" (Abercrombie, 1990, p. 99). Remember that Le Corbusier designed geometric wallpaper patterns during the 1930s; Mies van der Rohe used heavily-patterned marble in many of his commissions; Wright is world renowned for his art glass windows; and Venturi applied surface decoration to his line of plywood furniture for Knoll.

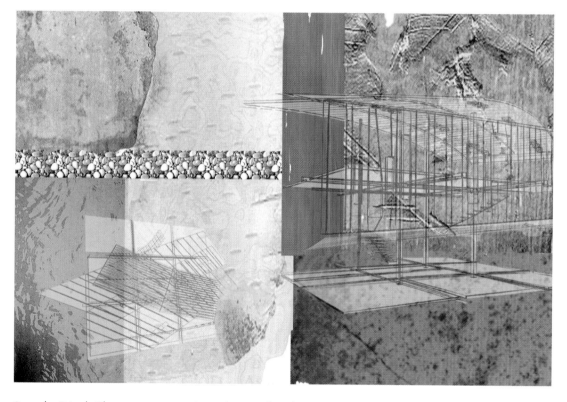

Sapsucker Woods Observatory, presentation and concept board

**Brian Davies**

CHAPTER 4

# Concepts

## Surface Qualities

Unlike decisions which are hidden within an object's structure, material selections provide an intimate visual and tactile connection to design. Every material has a surface appearance: the rough texture of stone, the smooth character of plastics, or the soft suppleness of leather. All of these examples are both visual and tactile in character. Some surface appearances are mostly visual. For example, polished marble, finished wood, or colorfully painted drywall are all relatively smooth to the touch but add a welcomed expression to our visual world.

While at the Bauhaus, Josef Albers taught a preliminary course on surface appearance. The subject received careful study by faculty and students, resulting in the definition of a tripart system for surface analysis: **structure, facture**, and **texture** (Albers, 1938). According to Albers, the *structure* of a raw material was revealed within its method of origin. For textiles, the structure is the weave; for wood, the structure is the grain and growth pattern; and for marble, the structure is the composite of minerals and ore. *Facture* refers to the manner in which the raw material has been physically, chemically, or mechanically processed. For example, granite may be polished or honed; metal may be polished, bent, punched, or painted; and textiles may be printed, dyed, crushed, or quilted. *Texture* was used as a general term to signify the presence of both structure and facture.

Our perception and preference for textured surfaces depend on several variables. **Scale** is the relative size of the texture pattern. Materials with a small-scaled surface texture should be viewed at a close distance and with adequate illumination. These concerns are less critical with materials possessing large-scaled textures. Textures with a prominent **direction** have the ability to elongate or shorten our perception of form. For example, a wall made of brick has a horizontal quality due to the repetition of brick courses and may appear longer than a plain wall of the same length. **Illumination** is an important factor in our ability to see the three-dimensional qualities of texture. Generally, uniform lighting can diminish the tactile quality of a surface's appearance, whereas light, which grazes the surface, will produce highlights and shadows from the relief so that the material's texture can be clearly understood. A final modifier to consider is the **distance** between the viewer and the textured material. From far away only the color of the building's facade is visible; however, on closer examination, its surface consists of thousands of coarsely textured bricks. These four factors act in tandem and thus are important elements to consider when selecting and applying materials to three-dimensional forms.

Today, computer applications allow the digital artist to experiment with both structural and factural qualities of any imaginable material. Adjustments in opacity, reflectance, pattern repetition and direction, and scale are just a few ways to define and manipulate digital materials via sophisticated rendering software. Custom materials, ranging from oxidized metal and wood shingles to oriental carpets and colorful textiles, can be obtained from commercial digital libraries or may be created by scanning photographs or actual materials, which are then collected and stored in a personal material library.

# Cognition

## Rendering Surfaces and Objects

Digitally rendering form and surface appearance depends on the individual software. **Wireframe** or **line rendering** is one of the simplest methods of representing a three-dimensional object (Figure 4-1). However, wireframe renderings are difficult for the viewer to understand because they display twice the number of lines (front and back) necessary for representation. Another limitation of wireframe renderings is the inability to retain realistic surface characteristics. **Continuous shading**, on the other hand, can employ variables of opacity, luminance, pattern, and texture, thus achieving greater scene realism (Figure 4-2).

Four shading modes exist in professional rendering programs: **flat, Gouraud, Phong**, and **metal**. Flat and Gouraud are simple shading methods and do not display cast shadows (Figure 4-3). For this reason, they are generally used for preliminary renderings and scenes which do not require a high level of realism. Phong is the most popular shading method for the digital artist. It produces sharp specular highlights and supports cast shadows, reflection maps, and

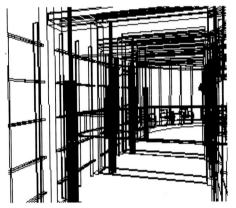

**Figure 4-1** ◀
Wireframe rendering
of interior

**Figure 4-2** ◀
Full-color, continuous
rendering of interior

▶ **Figure 4-3**

Example of simple
flat shading

▶ **Figure 4-4**

Example of metal
shading, resulting in
greater realism

other material properties (Figure 4-4). Metal is a special shading mode used to produce a metallic effect on objects with designated materials. Like Phong, metal shading supports cast shadows and other mapping capabilities.

All surface patterns and textures used in digital rendering consist of **pixels**. Short for picture element, a pixel is the smallest unit of an image. "Image" is quite a broad term in computer graphics; it can refer to a complex scene or to something as simple as the letter A. Hundreds of pixels arranged along a

matrix grid are needed to create a single image, also called a **bitmap**. The more pixels used to create a bitmap image, the finer the detail (Figure 4-5). Resolution of a bitmap image is defined by the number of horizontal pixels divided by the number of vertical pixels. This is referred to as a bitmap's **aspect ratio**.

**Figure 4-5**

Bitmap enlarged to show individual pixels

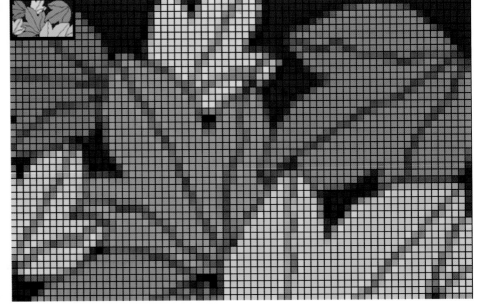

Bitmap images are created using various kinds of two-dimensional graphic software packages, such as Photoshop, Paintbrush, Animator Pro, and Fractal Painter. Different software and hardware manufacturers have developed many image file formats, some of which are listed here:

| | |
|---|---|
| BMP | Generic Windows bitmap |
| CEL | Animator Pro proprietary format |
| GIF | Graphic Interchange format |
| TIF | Tagged Image File format |
| TGA | Targa format |
| JPEG | Joint Photographic Experts Group |
| PCX | Paint proprietary format |
| PSD | Photoshop proprietary format |

Differences between file formats center on resolution and portability. CEL and BMP files typically have lower resolutions, while TIF and TGA formats are known for their high image quality. Note that file size is proportionally related to resolution; the higher the resolution, the larger the file size. The TIF format is supported by both Macintosh and Windows applications, making it the most popular file type for transferring images between platforms and graphics programs. JPEG files are commonly used on the Internet but have less stable resolution quality than other file formats.

Material libraries are made up of hundreds of files using many of the formats noted above. Default libraries included with individual rendering applications adequately represent the most common surface materials, such as wood, marble, and polished metal. However, to rely exclusively on a software's default library limits the designers' creative choices. Therefore, most digital artists create their own personal digital libraries. Customizing a material library is a relatively simple process. One method requires the purchase of a digital library from a reputable software vendor. Once loaded onto the computer's hard drive, the new bitmap images merge with the default material library to work seamlessly with the rendering application. The second method used to customize an existing library is to produce your own bitmap files by scanning. Scanners (flat-bed and slide) are easy to use and, with recent technological advances, are quite affordable for the independent digital artist. Scanning software is provided by the hardware manufacturer and includes options to change the original photograph's color, orientation, and scale. One benefit of scanning over purchasing ready-made libraries is the ability to control image content and quality.

## Mapping Surface Texture

A material's structural, factural, and textural qualities are controlled through the use of **mapping coordinates**. Mapping coordinates enable the digital artist to apply a 2D picture (bitmapped image) onto a 3D object. Maps are required for all digital materials which have an optical pattern or tactile surface texture. Different types of maps perform different functions. Planar, cylindrical, and spherical maps control a surface texture's location, orientation, scale, and repetition. **Planar** mapping is used to apply a bitmap image to a flat

**Figure 4-6** ◄

Mapping types:
planar, cylindrical,
and spherical

object, such as a wall or floor. **Cylindrical** and **spherical** maps are used to wrap a bitmap image around a curved surface (Figure 4-6). The next group of maps defines a material's surface color, optical, and tactile qualities. **Texture** maps essentially "paint" a bitmap picture onto the surface of an object. Texture maps are commonly used to create wood grain, marble veining, and textile patterns (Figure 4-7). **Opacity** maps control the level of a surface's transparency. **Bump** maps alter the surface normals of an object to create an embossed effect. **Specular** maps are used to project a bitmap image within the specular highlight of an object. **Reflection** maps are used to create the effect of a mirrored surface (Figure 4-8). Complex materials may require several maps to produce a desired rendering effect. Note that many of these special mapping features require Phong or metal rendering modes.

▶**Figure 4-7**
Wood and camou-
flage texture maps
applied to geometry

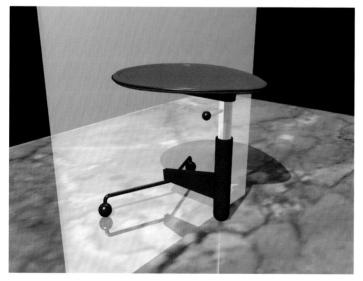

▶**Figure 4-8**
Result of a reflection
map applied to the
marble floor

# Applications

## Digital Sample Board with 3D Studio VIZ

The following hands-on tutorial will give you experience in creating, manipulating, and applying surface materials to a wireframe model of a traditional sample board (Figure 4-9).

**Figure 4-9**
Tutorial: final, rendered material board

**TIP**

*The software 3D Studio VIZ and 3D Studio MAX are almost identical in command structure and features. Users with MAX should be able to complete this entire tutorial even though it was written using VIZ.*

**TIP**

*When opening file formats other than MAX, such as DWG, DXF, or 3DS, you must use the FILE\ Import command.*

Begin by initializing the 3D Studio VIZ or MAX program. Load the file called **SAM-PLEBD.MAX** which contains a wireframe model of a material sample board. To accomplish this, use the **FILE\Open** command.

You will find the file under the CH4 subdirectory on the enclosed CD. Once located, click on the filename and then on **Open** to complete the loading process. After a few seconds, the wireframe model should become visible in all four viewports, top, front, left, and camera (Figure 4-10). Like viewing a surface at night without any illumination, rendering this wireframe model without lights would produce an environment of dark gray and black tones. Therefore, omnidirectional lights and spotlights have already been included in the file for this exercise. For more information about lighting, refer to Chapter 5.

Your screen should contain four command systems: a pull-down menu bar along the top of the screen, a toolbar, command panels in the upper right, and the status-and-prompt line at

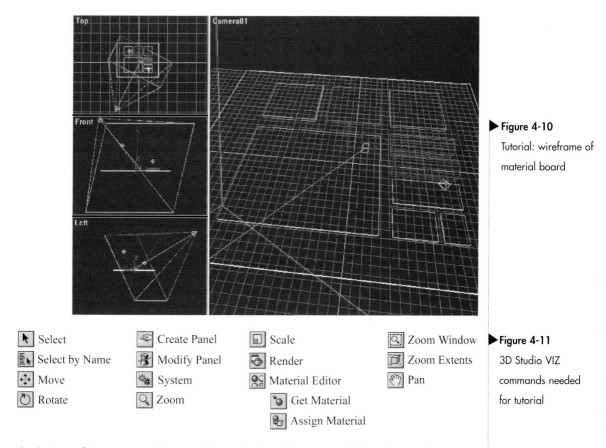

▶Figure 4-10

Tutorial: wireframe of

material board

| | | | |
|---|---|---|---|
| ▮ Select | ▮ Create Panel | ▮ Scale | ▮ Zoom Window |
| ▮ Select by Name | ▮ Modify Panel | ▮ Render | ▮ Zoom Extents |
| ▮ Move | ▮ System | ▮ Material Editor | ▮ Pan |
| ▮ Rotate | ▮ Zoom | ▮ Get Material | |
| | | ▮ Assign Material | |

▶Figure 4-11

3D Studio VIZ

commands needed

for tutorial

the bottom of the screen. Before working with the subject area of this chapter, familiarize yourself with the location of commands and icons which will be used in this tutorial (Figure 4-11). Like other Windows applications, 3D Studio VIZ has the Undo, Clone (Copy), and Delete commands located under the Edit menu.

For this first exercise, mapping coordinates have already been assigned to the model. You will learn how to apply materials using two methods. The first and easiest is called drag-and-drop. The second method uses the Material Editor to assign materials to selected objects.

In the camera viewport, use the **Selection** (arrow) tool to pick on upper right wireframe object (square). When selected, the object should display a red X,Y coordinate icon. Move to the command panel (top right), and pick on the **CREATE\System** command. Next, click on the **Drag** button and a list of folders will appear. Double-click on the **Textures** folder to

▶TIP

*When in doubt*
*about any command*
*or feature, consult*
*the HELP menu at*
*the top of the screen.*
*To locate commands*
*and buttons on the*
*screen, access the*
*Contents\User*
*Interface section of*
*the HELP menu.*

**TIP** ◀

*By right-clicking on a viewport's name, several shading options become available: Wireframe, Flat, and Smooth and Highlight. Note that these are simple shading formats for display purposes only. They should not be equated with the high-quality, full-color rendering capabilities achieved by using the Rendering command.*

open. View all of the material bitmaps displayed by using the scroll arrows. Use the mouse to click on a material's name. Hold down on the mouse button, drag the highlighted material onto the camera viewport, and position the cursor over the previously selected object. Note that the cursor icon changes shape as it moves over the selected object. Release the mouse button to apply the chosen material to the object. Repeat using the same material for all objects on the sample board except for the top center square.

The next step will enable you to see the materials you've just assigned. Select the command **RENDERING\Render** from the top menu (or use the Render tool). A dialogue box appears. Accept all defaults and pick on the **Render** button at the bottom of the box. The rendering process will take between 15 and 30 seconds depending on the internal speed of your computer. Note that the same assigned material appears differently because of variations to the mapping coordinates. To exit, click on the **X** at the top right corner of the render viewport.

Drag-and-drop contains only a small number of digital materials. To see the full default library of VIZ, you must explore the Materials Editor. Begin by clicking on the **Material Editor** tool, the icon with four colored spheres at the upper right of the screen. A dialogue box appears with six rendered spheres, another toolbar, and roll-out commands (Figure 4-12). Click on the **Get Material** button. The Material/Map Browser dialogue box appears; click on **BROWSE FROM\Material Library** and then **FILE\Open** the **3DSVIZ.MAT** file. Scroll through the list of materials (materials have a blue sphere prior to their names; maps have a green icon). As you find one of interest, click on the name, then **OK**. The selected material will appear in place of the first sphere. Repeat by clicking on the **Get Material** button.

Now its time to apply one of the materials in the Material Editor to the sample board. Make sure that an object is selected in the camera viewport (use the Selection tool). In the Material Editor click on the **Assign Material to Selection** button (third from the left, just below the six rendered spheres). Exit or reduce the Material Editor. Use the **RENDERING\Render** command to evaluate the applied materials. Continue to experiment. The sample board image, shown at the beginning of this exercise, used the following materials from top left to right: tile0011.tga, blue fabric, blue bumpy cloth, benediti.tga, chrome, copper, teak.tga, floor raised disc, ashen.tga. (Note that the materials ending with a .tga are those applied by the drag-and-drop method.)

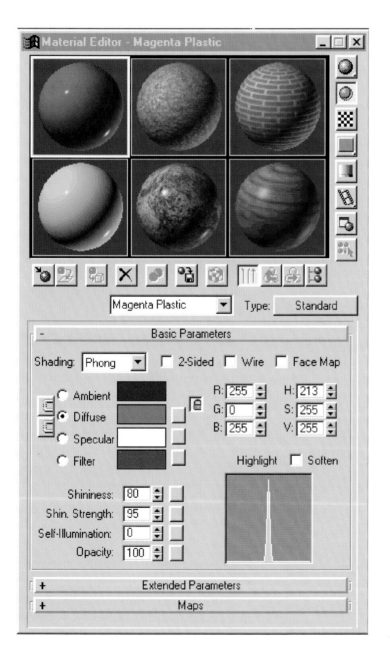

▶**TIP**

*To change the display from a sphere to a cube or cylinder, click and hold on the top sphere tool icon to the right of the rendered spheres. Use the cube to display materials intended for flat surfaces, such as floors and walls. Change the background display by picking on the checkerboard icon. Use this background when displaying transparent or translucent materials.*

## Mapping

**TIP** ◀

*Remove mapping coordinates when they are no longer needed for rendering a scene. Maps are not necessary for (1) reflection and refraction materials, (2) three-dimensional procedural maps, (3) face mapped materials, and (4) unpatterned, untextured materials.*

Controlling a material's orientation, direction, scale, and pattern repetition is accomplished through mapping coordinates. This software uses three methods to apply mapping coordinates: (1) select Generate Mapping Coordinates option when creating geometric primitives, (2) apply a UVW Map Modifier to existing geometry, or (3) use special controls associated with the lofting process. Using the Generate Mapping Coordinates default option does not give the digital artist control over a material's character. To affect variables of scale, orientation, and location, use the UVW Map Modifier option.

### UVW Map Modifier

Bitmaps, such as wood, brick, or fabric, are 2D images later applied to a 3D form. A UVW map modifier provides control over how the 2D bitmap relates to the geometry and parallels the relative direction of XYZ coordinates. Begin by evoking the command **MODIFY\UVW Map**. Five choices are available under *Parameters*: planar, cylindrical, spherical, shrink wrap, and box. Because the objects on the sample board are simple, rectangular forms, you will use the Box option. Remember, to make any modifications to an object, you must first select the geometry. Select **Box** and notice that the orange mapping coordinates (called a gizmo) changes proportion and conforms to the size of the selected object. Click on each of the four remaining mapping types to view their mapping shape. Return to the Box option.

**TIP** ◀

*The short yellow line on the gizmo (planar, spherical, or shrink wrap) indicates the top of the map. For cylindrical and spherical maps, the green edge shows where the two edges of the map meet to form a seam.*

To change the size, location, or orientation of the gizmo, click on the **Sub-Object** button in the *Modifier Stack*. The map changes color from an orange to a yellow gizmo. Not accessing the Sub-Object feature would result in subsequent commands being performed on the geometry instead of the mapping gizmo. Use the **Move, Rotate**, or **Scale** tools to manipulate the mapping coordinates. Render the camera viewport to review changes to the applied materials in the digital scene.

Six other mapping options exist under **MODIFY\Parameters\Alignment.** *Fit* centers the gizmo and resizes the map to match the proportions of the selected geometry. *Center* moves the gizmo to the object's center. *Bitmap Fits* resizes the map to match a specified bitmap image. *Normals Align* orients the map toward an object's designated face. Use the mouse to select the appropriate face. *Reset* returns the gizmo to its default settings. *Acquire* copies the mapping coordinates from other geometry in the scene. Try the **Fit, Center**, and **Reset** features. Render the camera viewport again to see the results of your changes to the mapping coordinates.

# Rendering an Interior Scene with 3D Studio VIZ

This next exercise focuses on (1) manipulating existing materials in the default library, (2) creating your own library of imported scanned images, and (3) applying these materials to a digital environment (Figure 4-13). Take a few minutes to review the commands and icons important for this tutorial (Figure 4-14).

▶ **TIP**

*Since mapped textures increase rendering time they should be used primarily for elements of design importance, and for objects located in the foreground. Use a solid material of similar coloring for items which provide background detail to the scene. For example, in a restaurant with many tables, only a few tables and chairs in the foreground need to be realistic, mapped materials.*

▶ **Figure 4-13**
Tutorial: final image of office interior

| | | |
|---|---|---|
| ▲ Select | ◈ Create Panel | ◔ Material Editor |
| ▤ Select by Name | ☁ Modify Panel | ◔ Get Material |
| ✢ Move | ▥ Display Panel | ▦ Assign Material |
| ↻ Rotate | ✳ System | ◈ Go to Parent |
| ▣ Scale | ◯ Zoom | ✖ Reset |
| ◹ Render | ▣ Zoom Window | |
| | ▢ Zoom Extents | |
| | ✋ Pan | |
| | Type: Standard | |

▶ **Figure 4-14**
3D Studio VIZ commands needed for tutorial

**TIP** ◀

*Hot materials are displayed in the Material Editor and have already been applied to the digital scene. They are identified by white bracketed corners in the display area. Making changes to a hot material in the Material Editor will affect the applied material in the scene. To create variations of a hot material without automatically updating it in the scene, use a copy of the material. Copy the material by selecting it with the mouse, holding, and dragging to another display slot. Give the copy a different name and then change its properties.*

If not already in 3D Studio VIZ, initialize the program. Open the file called **INTERIOR.MAX** which contains a wireframe model of an interior space. To do this, use the **FILE\Open** command. Find the file under the CH4 subdirectory on the enclosed CD. After a few seconds, a wireframe of a room should appear in all four viewports on the screen (Figure 4-15). Again, lighting and some maps are already included for you within this file.

### Material Editor

Because many of the materials available in the default library are not representative of colors and patterns found in the interior environment, the digital artist will need to create a custom library. Click on the **Material Editor** tool and make one of the six spheres current. The current material will be indicated with a heavy white border. You will alter this color by manipulating its Ambient, Diffuse, and Specular settings. With the mouse, click on **Basic Parameters\Ambient** swatch to activate the Color Selection dialogue box. Adjust the color by varying the HSV and RGB sliders; respond by clicking on the **Close** button when you are satisfied with the new Ambient color. Repeat for the Diffuse and Specular settings. Give the new material a name by typing it in the Name field below the Material Editor toolbar. Repeat to create four new materials.

To save the materials just created, click on the **Put to Library** tool. Repeat for all new materials. Use the **Get Material\Browse From\Material Editor** command to verify that the new materials exist by their given names. Apply these new materials to the sofa (back, seat, and bolster) by using the **Put Material to Scene** tool. Remember that the object must be selected in order to apply materials to its geometry. Render the camera viewport to assess the newly created materials.

### Advanced Rendering Features

Up until now, you have only manipulated solid-colored, opaque materials in the Material Editor. You will now experiment with other features to create materials with greater realism. In the Material Editor, make a material current. Using the mouse, adjust the **Shininess** numeric value. Click on the material display slot with your mouse; notice the change to the highlight. High shininess values produce an illusion of gloss; smaller values simulate a dull,

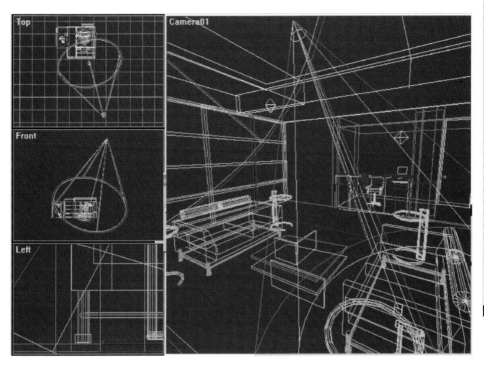

Tutorial: wireframe of office interior

matte surface finish. Next, experiment with the **Shin. Strength** option. Adjusting this feature will vary the intensity (brilliance) of the highlight. Click on the material to see the surface change. *Self-Illumination* simulates the effect of a bright light source shining from within. This option works well when trying to represent a glowing lamp or the distant sun. The **Opacity** feature varies the transparency of a surface material. Adjust the value and click on the display to evaluate the change.

The Wire button is located to the right of the shading mode. Using this option changes the material from a continuous rendered surface to a colored wireframe. Click on the **Wire** button to experiment with this feature. (If cast shadows are desired from a wireframe material, you must use spotlights with the ray-tracing option; see Chapter 5.)

The 2-Sided button is located just to the left of the Wire button. This feature renders both the interior and exterior sides of an object. It is used primarily to (1) improve the realism of transparent and wire materials, and (2) to override inverted normals. Normals aid in the rendering process by indicating the orientation of an object's surface faces. If a wireframe object appears in the viewport but will not render, its normals are probably reversed, as represented by the left seat cushion (Figure 4-16). Creating and assigning a 2-Sided material to an object is an easy way of correcting rendering problems associated with misoriented normals. Note that 2-Sided materials should be used sparingly as they will double rendering time.

Create several new materials using the advanced techniques demonstrated above. Remember to name each new material by entering it in the name field. Apply these new materials to objects in the digital model. Render the camera viewport to evaluate your work.

**Figure 4-16** ◀
Reversed normals on
left seat cushion

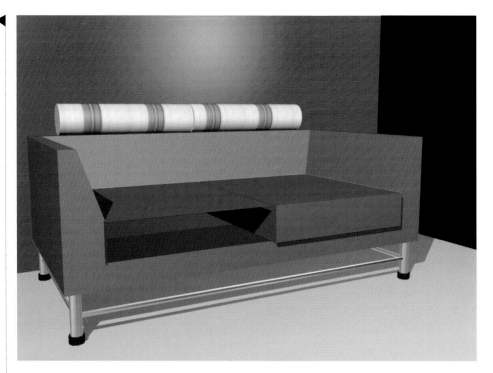

## Bitmap Features

Although adequate to render many surface types, default libraries may not represent specialized materials needed for an individual project. Therefore, additional bitmap files may be purchased from a vendor or created by scanning. For this demonstration, it is assumed that your have already scanned a patterned textile fabric, called FABRIC.JPG, and have copied it into the Maps subdirectory of 3D Studio VIZ.

Return to the Material Editor and click on the Maps roll-out bar to display more options. Note the eleven rows of buttons and controls which enable the digital artist to modify bitmapped materials (Figure 4-17). Move your mouse along the second row (Diffuse) stopping at the column called Map. Click on the **None** button to display additional features. Click on the **Type** button (located just beneath the *Go To Parent* tool) to recall the Material/Map Browser

▶ **TIP**

*Bitmaps for rendering custom materials must appear in the Maps subdirectory. Save a copy of all custom image files used in a project and store with the project files to ensure accurate renderings in the future.*

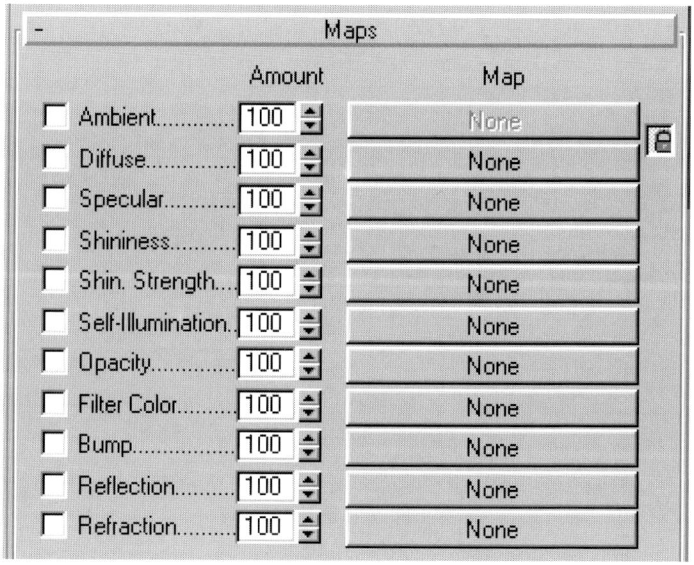

▶ **Figure 4-17**
Maps roll-out in 3D Studio VIZ

▶ **TIP**

*If you become lost in the sequence of commands above, use the Reset Material Settings tool in the Material Editor and begin again.*

dialogue box. Select **Browse From: New\Bitmap** and respond **OK**. With your mouse, click in the Bitmap field (located under the Bitmap parameters roll-out) and click on the file called **FABRIC.JPG** in the Maps subdirectory (Figure 4-18). Respond with **OK**. Use the **Go to Parent** tool to move to the top of this material's hierarchy. Name the material and apply to the area rug in the scene (select object by using the **Select by Name** tool). Render the camera viewport to evaluate the new material.

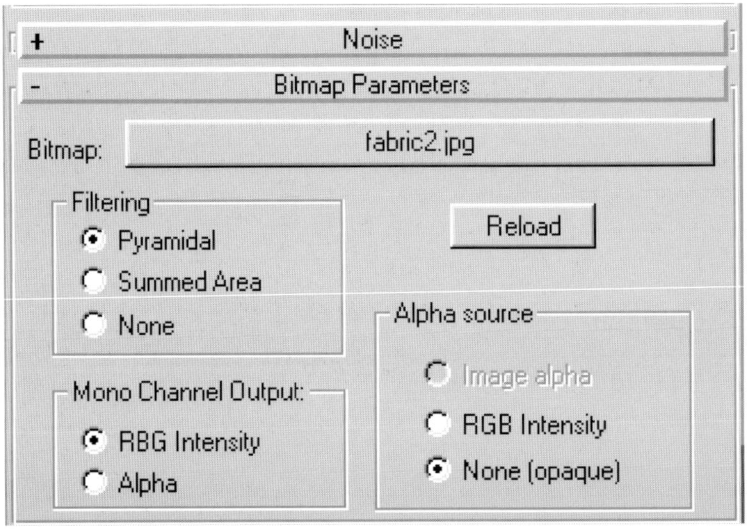

**Figure 4-18** ◀

Bitmap parameters
roll-out in
3D Studio VIZ

**TIP** ◀

*To remove a map
from a material,
pick, hold and drag
a None button from
another slot over the
map slot you no
longer want; release
mouse.*

You will now give the current material a tactile quality by adding a bump map. Use the **Go To Parent** tool to return to the *Maps roll-out*. Locate the row called Bump; move your mouse to the right stopping at the column called Map. Click on the **None** button. The Material/Map Browser dialogue box appears. Select **Browse From: New\Bitmap**; finish by clicking on **OK**. In the *Bitmap Parameters* roll-out, click in the Bitmap field and choose a map whose tactile pattern is familiar, such as brick (**BRICKBMP.TIF**) or beebees (**BEEBEES.JPG**). Return to the *Maps* rollout (Go To Parent tool) and increase the **Amount** value setting to 100. Click in the material display slot. Study how the bump map has changed the surface characteristics of the material. Apply this material to the area rug in the scene and render the camera viewport. Unfortunately, at this distance the bump texture is barely visible. However, zoom in the camera viewport to get a closer look at the texture.

The final phase of this exercise will demonstrate how to create a realistic wood floor. You will be manipulating the mapping coordinates to simulate tongue-and-groove wood strip flooring. Begin by selecting the object called **Floor1**. Next, use the command **DISPLAY\Hide by Selection\Hide Unselected**. A wireframe of only the floor remains displayed. Use **MODIFY\UVW Mapping\Parameters\Box** to define mapping coordinates for the floor. Return to the Material Editor and use the **Get Material** tool to choose *Wood Ashen*. Apply the material to the selected object (Floor1). Render the camera viewport. The scale of the bitmapped image is too large and distorted. Exit the render viewport and return to **MODIFY\UVW Mapping\Mapping Parameters**. Change the **V Tile** value from 0 to 15. Render again. Unhide all the components of the model by using the **DISPLAY\Unhide All** command. Render once again to evaluate the entire interior scene.

Before exiting, save the materials you created by saving them to a personal material library. Use the **Get Material** tool to return to the **Material\Map Browser** dialogue box. Select **Browse From: Scene**, and then **File: Save As**. Type your name (or the project name) in the area provided. Note that material libraries for both 3D Studio VIZ and 3D Studio MAX end with a .max extension.

## Summary

Texture and surface appearance, whether real or implied, visually communicates the kind of value placed on design quality, performance, and beauty. Sometimes these qualities are difficult to evaluate in small material samples. Other times its hard to imagine how a specific material will feel in a different color palette, a larger scale, or once applied to three-dimensional form. How better to visualize these traditional shortcomings than with the aide of computer graphics and a greater sense of realism?

▶ **TIP**

*In a complex scene, it is sometimes difficult to physically select an individual object, such as a spotlight's target. Use the Selected By Name tool (top toolbar) to alphabetically display all the objects in the scene. You may now easily select an object by its name.*

Office lobby, two views

**Strang Inc.**

# ILLUMINATING YOUR VIRTUAL ENVIRONMENT

**5**

*Light is a powerful source in our visual world. Whether natural or artificial, it gives warmth and character to a favorite room. Light may perform as an actor in a movie or Broadway play; it can add a sense of drama to a still photograph. Digital light can provide these same qualities to a virtual world.*

*Shadows, like highlights, await the designer's artistic touch, to be cast into the environment in a calligraphy of patterned light and shade.*
*- L. Michel*

Chapter written by Professor Kathleen Gibson.

# Introduction

Light wavelengths are not normally visible to us, and therefore we only "see" light when it interacts with a solid, gas, or liquid. Surface characteristics have an important impact on the quality of light we experience. For example, texture, transparency, and color can affect how we perceive and interpret illumination in our environment. Most people recognize that meaningful spaces require more than just basic illumination. Successful architects and designers embrace and creatively use light as a primary element in their design solutions. Think of some of the most renowned cathedrals in the world. Playful patterns of colored light stream in through large areas of stained-glass windows. The Chapel of Notre-Dame-du-Haut at Ronchamp, by Le Corbusier, quickly comes to mind with its colorful, cylindrical shafts of light. Other environments have limited access to natural light and therefore must discover creative ways to use artificial light. Architect Helmut Jahn, at Chicago's O'Hare Airport, used colorful ribbons of neon to add energy and motion to a lifeless pedestrian concourse (Figure 5-1).

**Figure 5-1** ◀
Playful use of artificial light in the Chicago-O'Hare airport concourse.

Outdoor pavilion, schematic model

**Cristina Malcolm**

# Concepts

## Natural and Artificial Light

Because light has become such a necessary component in everyday life, little thought is given to its character and behavior. Its quality varies considerably, which in turn affects the visual character of the surrounding environment. For example, contrast your bright work environment with that of a candlelit dining room. Successful lighting solutions evolve out of a knowledge of basic lighting principles, understanding of product performance, and creative vision.

### Lighting Principles

The way light falls on an object is governed by the principles of physics. Although light may appear complex to the novice designer, there is a logic and a consistency to its behavior. When light waves strike a 3D object, they produce a light area, an attached shadow, and a cast shadow (Figure 5-2). **Attached shadows** appear on the surface of an object as it faces away from the light source. The less illumination a surface receives from the light source, the darker it appears. These gradual changes in value help the viewer understand an object's form and contours. The angle relative to the light source is called the **angle of incidence**. A surface is brightly illuminated when the angle of incidence is 90°; deviation from 90° will result in a lower level of light intensity. **Cast shadows** are projected onto other surfaces by an object located directly in the path of light. The quality and size of a cast shadow depend on the individual light source. Bright, intense light creates dark shadows with crisp edges. Lower levels of light will create softer, less dramatic shadows. Its size is a factor of the location and direction of the light source. Light placed directly above an object will cast a small shadow, similar to the sun at noon. Dramatic shadows appear when the light source is located at an oblique angle to the object (Figure 5-3). Some **reflected** light will appear in the area of the attached shadow caused by light bouncing off other objects nearby. Objects with a **highly lustered** surface will reflect light in only one direction, causing the surface to behave as a mirror. **Matte** surfaces randomly scatter reflected light in all directions, producing a dull effect. Areas of intense brightness are called **highlights** and together with shadow provide important depth cues for the viewer.

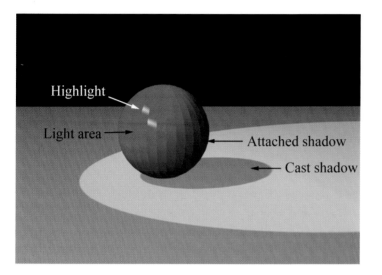

Highlight

Light area

Attached shadow

Cast shadow

▶ **Figure 5-2**
Behavior of light on a
spherical form

▶ **Figure 5-3**
Direction of light
affects attached and
cast shadows

**Product Performance**

How light performs in the environment is controlled by its **distribution, direction**, and **color**. These three variables are the easiest to control and manipulate when designing a lighting solution for a residence or place of employment. Distribution can be categorized as either **general, local,** or **accent**; however, many environments contain a lighting solution using all three. General illumination, sometimes called **ambient**, creates a uniform distribution of light and is commonly used in offices and schools. Because of the uniformity of general lighting, spaces are consistently bright and active. Local illumination, also called **task** lighting, focuses its distribution toward areas where detailed activities occur. Task lighting is commonly found under kitchen cabinets, over a writing desk, or near a seating area. Accent lighting is used to highlight a special building feature, illuminate art, or to add visual interest through patterns of light. Retail stores and restaurants use accent lighting to create unique displays and add an inviting atmosphere for their customers.

The direction of light is controlled by a light fixture, which manipulates the rays of light. Fixtures can focus light downward, upward, or in various directions, referred to as multidirectional. Downlights provide direct illumination to horizontal surfaces below, causing them to become bright, while the ceiling plane and vertical surfaces remain relatively dark. Uplights produce a softer, indirect illumination, while concentrating bright light on the ceiling and vertical surfaces. Because multidirectional fixtures deliver light in several directions, they are used primarily to achieve a high-luminance, uniform lighting solution.

Visible light consists of seven wavelengths containing the following colors: red, orange, yellow, green, blue, indigo, and violet. Appropriate amounts of each wavelength together produce what is called **white light**, that is, light which appears to be colorless. Not all artificial lamps can adequately replicate white light. **Incandescent** lamps are excellent at rendering warm colors but show less support for blue. **Fluorescent** tubes are known to offer less color rendition of deep reds and blue-greens. However, because of the efficiency and popularity of fluorescent lamps, manufacturers have treated some tubes with a phosphor coating, resulting in output which nearly replicates the incandescent color spectrum (i.e., deluxe warm or daylight fluorescents). Other kinds of lamps, such as mercury, high-pressure sodium, and multivapor, have unbalanced color spectrums and are generally not used in interior spaces.

## Creative Vision

Choosing, specifying, and organizing lighting fixtures is the responsibility of a design professional. According to expert lighting designers Smith and Bertolone (1986), creating a successful lighting scheme requires four key elements: (1) framing, (2) primary focus, (3) secondary focus, and (4) delight. For sake of argument, let's use a dining facility to test their recommended elements for lighting design. Framing would be used to exclude irrelevant visual information by focusing the customer's attention away from the kitchen and servicing areas. The greatest level of illumination in the space should be the primary focus. In our example, the hostess area and bar are the primary foci. The secondary focus receives the second brightest lighting treatment and is used to visually balance the primary focus. Intimate illumination at each table will be the secondary focus in our dining example. As noted, memorable lighting solutions have at least one unusual or unexpected feature - delight. Our dining room uses accent lighting to highlight a prized collection of imported wine.

Digital software can be a useful tool for designers and architects to visually explore and analyze optimum lighting conditions. Knowledge of the physical characteristics of light will aid the digital artist in creating a realistic virtual environment. Light distribution, direction, and color are easily defined and controlled using features offered by many digital rendering packages. Design experimentation is encouraged by the software's interface, which allows constructing and rendering of shadow patterns within minutes. Note that some commercial applications are highly technical and provide accurate photometric and scientific data, but they usually have limited color-rendering capabilities. Other sophisticated rendering packages may offer only approximations of the characteristics and behavior of natural and artificial light. Careful analysis and project objectives must be determined by the digital artist prior to the purchase of rendering software for lighting design and simulation.

# Cognition

## Rendering Digital Light

To achieve a sense of realism, many software applications have been created to simulate the natural behavior of light and shadow. Professional rendering programs offer numerous methods for the digital artist to create and manipulate the characteristics of light and shadow within an entire scene. Luminous representations may be created through (1) the selection of a shading mode, (2) the definition of an object's material, or (3) an individual light source. In most cases, all three options are needed to create a sense of realism.

Four shading modes exist in professional rendering programs: flat, Gouraud, Phong, and metal. **Flat** and **Gouraud** are simple shading methods and do not display cast shadows (Figure 5-4). For this reason, they are generally used for preliminary renderings and scenes which do not require a high level of realism. **Phong** is the most popular shading method for the digital artist. It produces sharp, specular highlights and supports cast shadows, reflection maps, and other material properties (Figure 5-5). **Metal** is a special shading mode used to produce a metallic effect on objects with designated surface materials. Like phong, metal shading supports cast shadows and other mapping capabilities.

**Figure 5-4** ◄

Example of simple flat shading

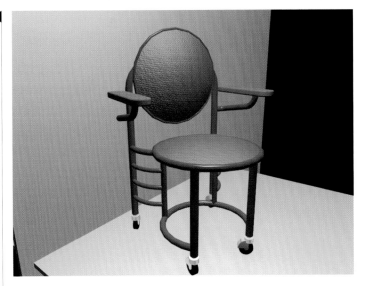

▶ **Figure 5-5**
Example of more
realistic, Phong
shading

There is much latitude in the creation of digital surface materials. Every digital material, whether blue plastic, amber glass, or brushed aluminum, is defined by three properties: ambient, diffuse, and specular reflections (Figure 5-6). **Ambient** reflection simulates the attached shadow of an object. It is generally a darker value of the diffuse hue but can be manipulated to represent another color reflected from a neighboring object. **Diffuse** reflection represents the hue in direct light. **Specular** reflection simulates the highlight, a bright spot of light reflected by a high-gloss surface material. Materials with patterns or texture may require a 2D bitmap and the use of mapping coordinates. (Refer to Chapters 3 and 4 for more detailed information on digital color and materials.)

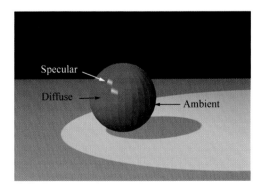

▶ **Figure 5-6**
Digital material
properties: ambient,
diffuse, and specular

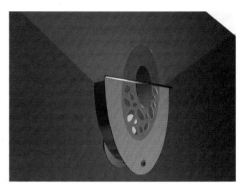

**Figure 5-7** ◀

Digital simulation of
light projecting from
a wall sconce

Finally, light and shadow can be controlled through an individual light source. The digital artist can adjust each lamp's color, brightness, distance, direction of beam, pattern of beam, and ability or inability to calculate cast shadows. **Omni** lights illuminate equally in all directions from the source, similar to the sun. However, unlike the sun, omni lights do not cast shadows. They are used primarily to provide general illumination within a digital environment. **Directional** lights create parallel, constant illumination in one direction similar to that of the sun (Figure 5-7). **Spotlights** radiate light in one direction from the light source and are used to create dramatic cast shadows within a scene. Defining shadow patterns are calculation-intensive and require a large amount of computer memory; therefore, spotlights in a digital environment should be used

**Figure 5-8** ◀

Key placement of
spotlights for
dramatic visual effect

with specific intent (Figure 5-8). **Ambient** light is used to simulate general, low-level, uniform illumination without any shadow. Color changes to ambient light are quite powerful and will affect the entire scene. For example, a dark blue ambient light may be used to simulate moonlight reflecting through an open window; a warm hue may simulate early evening light cast from a beautiful sunset. Note that with ambient light, no light source or direction is defined.

## The Interaction of Digital Light

Computer programs give an amazing amount of control to the digital artist in the area of lighting. As with the artificial light discussed above, simulating illumination in a virtual environment requires the ability to manipulate the light's direction, distribution, and color. The definition of a light's position in space and the direction in which it casts is easily controlled through coordinates (X,Y,Z). Some applications require a specific numeric location; however, most rendering programs enable the digital artist to easily "drag and drop" lights into the scene. Downlight, uplight, and multidimensional lighting solutions found in the natural world are relatively easy to replicate using the computer. A light's distribution is controlled through three parameters associated with spotlights: hotspot, falloff, and shape. A **hotspot** is an area with bright, even illumination (Figure 5-9). Tightly confined hotspots create a constrained, directed beam of light; large hotspots simulate a more diffuse distribution of light. A gradual dissipation of illumination is controlled by the **falloff** parameter. Using a falloff softens a spotlight's hard edge produced by the hotspot settings. The **shape** of a digital light can be either round, to simulate the distribution from an incandescent fixture, or rectangular, to simulate the distribution from a fluorescent fixture.

▶ **Figure 5-9**
Hotspot and falloff features define a shadow's edge

A digital lamp's hue is manipulated by adjusting the RGB and HLS color gamuts. Simulating the sun or an incandescent source requires a yellow-white light, whereas stage lighting in a theatrical scene will require lights of primary blue, red, and green to portray a sense of realism.

Creating a realistic scene depends not only on the quality and color of light, but also the character of the surface material which it encounters. For example, a material with a low **transparency** setting is nearly opaque. As the transparency setting increases, the amount of light passing through the material also increases, allowing objects beyond to become visible (Figure 5-10). Materials which appear to glow from within, such as a bright pink neon tube, are created by manipulating a material's **luminance**. Creating realistic lighting simulations is not limited to the software's lighting options. As in nature, it is a unique combination of light interacting with the surface characteristics of various materials. (See Chapter 4 for more detailed information on defining materials.)

Two final rendering features have an impact on digital lighting: **attenuation** and **radiosity**. Attenuation decreases illumination on objects farther away from the light source. This feature is especially effective in communicating distance in outdoor scenes. Attenuation is controlled through the individual light source. Radiosity is the term given to light reflected off the surface of an object. Mirrored objects in highly realistic digital scenes are the result of ray-tracing operations. (See Chapter 7 for tutorials using advanced rendering features.

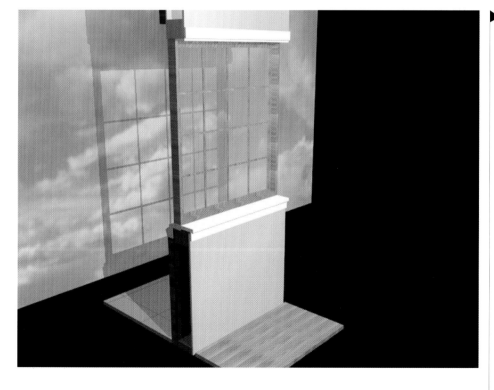

▶ **Figure 5-10**
Ray tracing enables
light to pass through
transparent materials

# Applications

## Lighting an Object with 3D Studio VIZ

The following hands-on tutorial will give you experience in creating and manipulating digital light on a piece of furniture (Figure 5-11). You will experience variations of lighting effects which will result in different qualities of shadow patterns cast onto neighboring surfaces.

**Figure 5-11 ◀**
Tutorial: final rendering of illuminated glass-top table

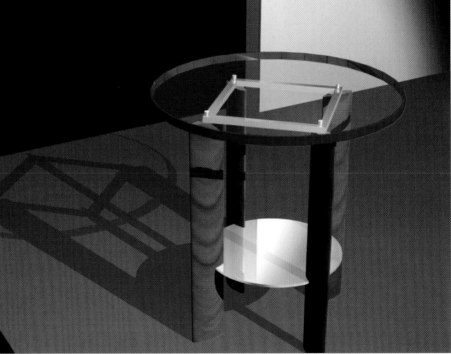

**TIP ◀**

*When in doubt about any command, consult the HELP menu at the top of the screen. To locate commands and buttons on the screen, access the Contents\User Interface section of the HELP menu.*

Begin by initializing the 3D Studio VIZ or MAX program. Load the file called **LIGHT-ING.MAX** which contains a wireframe model of a table. To do this, use the command **FILE\Open**. You will find the file located within the CH5 subdirectory on the enclosed CD. Once it is located, click on the filename and then on Open to complete the loading process. After a few seconds, a wireframe model of a table should become visible in all four viewports: top, front, left, and camera (Figure 5-12).

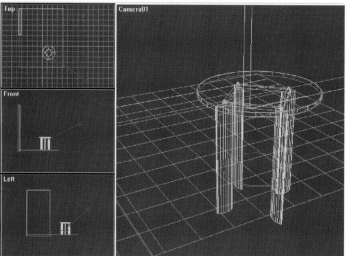

| | |
|---|---|
| ▶ | Select |
| ▶ | Select by Name |
| ✛ | Move |
| ⟳ | Render |
| ✎ | Create Panel |
| ⚒ | Modify Panel |
| ⚡ | Lights |
| 🔍 | Zoom |
| 🔍 | Zoom Window |
| ▢ | Zoom Extents |
| ✋ | Pan |

▶ **Figure 5-12**

Tutorial: wireframe

of table

▶ **Figure 5-13**

3D Studio VIZ

commands needed

for tutorial

▶ **TIP**

*When no lights are*
*specified for the*
*scene, 3D Studio*
*VIZ automatically*
*uses default lighting.*
*Shading with default*
*lighting results in a*
*lower quality image.*
*To achieve a higher*
*level of realism in*
*your scene, add sev-*
*eral omnidirectional*
*lights and spotlights*
*to your model. As*
*the first digital light*
*is placed into the*
*model, the default*
*setting is turned off*
*and the scene is illu-*
*minated only by the*
*lights you define.*

Your screen should contain four command systems: a pull-down menu bar along the top of the screen (toolbar) command panels along the right margin, the status-prompt line, and navigational tools at the bottom of the screen. Before working with the subject in this chapter, familiarize yourself with the location of commands and icons which will be used throughout this tutorial (Figure 5-13). As with other Windows applications, 3D Studio VIZ has the *Undo*, *Clone* (Copy), and *Delete* commands located under the EDIT menu.

## Omnidirectional Lights

Rendering this scene without lights, like viewing a room at night without any illumination, will produce an environment of dark gray and black tones. Therefore, your first objective is to add an omni light to this scene.

Begin by using the command series **CREATE\\*Lights*\\*Omni*** which is located on the command panel along the right margin. Accept all defaults, and in the plan viewport click with the mouse to the left of the table but still within the floor (orange) plane. One yellow (sometimes white) omni light appears in the scene. Note by looking in the front or left viewport that the omni light is on or below the ground plane. To raise the omni light in the scene,

TIP ◀

*Omni lights are multidirectional, casting light in all directions. They work best for adding general illumination.*

click first on the **Select** (arrow) tool and then within the left viewport. Next, click on the omni light once with your mouse. A red X,Y coordinates icon will appear noting that the object (omni light) is selected. Use the **Move** tool (double set of arrows) to relocate the light (click, hold, and drag) to a position above the height of the nearby wall. Click within the camera view to make it current. Render the scene using the **RENDERING\*Render** command (or Teapot icon) from the top pull-down menu. A dialogue box will appear. Accept all defaults and click on the **Render** button. The rendering process will take about 30 seconds. Study the image. Note that although some colors and textures are present, the vertical surfaces are relatively dark and no cast shadows are visible along the floor plane. Close the rendering by clicking on the **X** in the upper right corner of the rendered viewport.

TIP ◀

*Remember that different types of lamps support different color spectrums: incandescent are warm, and fluorescent tend to be cool. To create a better sense of realism in your digital scene, adjust the digital light sources to emulate the character of natural and artificial light sources which occur in the physical environment.*

Next, experiment with the color and brightness of the omni light. First, click on the omni light with your mouse. Remember that a red X, Y coordinates icon should appear attached to denote that the omni light has been selected. Access the **MODIFY** command panel. Scroll down to the *General Parameters*. Under *Color*, click on the gray box located between *On* and *Exclude*. A Color Selector dialogue box appears. Adjust the color and value with the slider bars or replace the numeric values for both RGB and HSV gamuts. Render the scene again to evaluate the changes made to the omni light.

Repeat the commands above to further experiment with color and omni lights. Practice manipulating the RGB sliders and the HSV sliders. Render again. (For more information about digital color principles, refer to Chapter 3.) When you have finished manipulating the omni light, return to the default settings: H=0, L=0, S=180, R=180, G=180, B=180.

## Spotlights, Shade, and Shadow

Spotlights are important because they create shadows and shadows provide depth cues, lending a sense of realism to a computer-generated image. Begin by using the **CREATE\*Lights\*Target Spot** command. In the command panel, scroll down to *Spotlight Parameters*. Pick on **Show Cone**; verify that *Circle* is selected. Move down to *Shadow Parameters*. Select **Cast Shadows** and **Use Shadow Maps**.

You will now define the X,Y,Z location of the spotlight and its direction. In the top (plan) viewport, use your mouse to click, hold, and drag. The first action (clicking) locates the light source in the scene. The second action and third action (holding and dragging) define the direction of the beam of light. Release the mouse to define the target. Study all four viewports. Notice in elevation

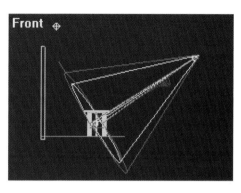

▶ **Figure 5-14**

Defining spotlight, hotspot, and falloff parameters

that the spotlight is at or below the ground plane. Use the **Move** tool (double arrows) located at middle top of the screen to reposition the light source. If further adjustment is needed, select on the spotlight's target in the front or left viewport to make it current. Then use the **Move** tool to change the target's position (Figure 5-14).

Verify that the camera viewport is current. Use the **RENDERING\Render** command to render the scene. Accept all defaults in the dialogue box. The rendering process will take a little longer than before. Shadow calculations increase rendering time. When you are finished, a full-color image should appear on your screen. Study the image for highlights and shadows. If shadows are not visible, check if you selected the **Cast Shadows** option in the *Shadows Parameters*. Close the rendering by clicking on the **X** in the upper right corner of the rendering viewport.

A rectangular spotlight will simulate a fluorescent fixture, whereas a circular shape best represents incandescent fixtures and the sun. Before proceeding, make sure that the target spot is selected. To adjust the shape of the light beam, return to the **MODIFY** panel and the *Spotlight Parameters*. Select **Rectangle**. View the spotlight's shape in the front and left viewports. Render the camera viewport to compare the beam spread. Return the spotlight's shape to a circle.

▶ **TIP**

*To scroll down the command panel, use the Pan (hand) tool in the lower right of the screen. To use, hold down the mouse and drag vertically down the command panel. Release the mouse when satisfied with the position. If the Pan tool is not displayed, make one of the orthographic viewports (top, front, left) current; this should return the Pan navigational tool to your screen.*

TIP ◀

*In a complex scene, it is sometimes difficult to physically select an individual object, such as a spotlight's target. Use the Selected By Name tool (top toolbar) to alphabetically display all the objects in the scene. You may now easily select an object by its name.*

You will now adjust the light's hotspot and falloff. The hotspot is a hard-edged area of intense brightness. A light's falloff is the area where light dissipates until it disappears into the darkness. Both qualities are easily controlled through **MODIFY\Spotlight Parameters.** Reduce the value of the hotspot and the falloff to about half of their present setting. Render the scene and assess the difference in the quantity of light and cast shadows.

One of the secrets of making a realistic scene lies in the quality of cast shadows as they project through transparent materials. 3D Studio VIZ offers two types of shadow rendering: shadow map and ray trace. Shadows created by using the shadow map option (default) are actually bitmaps projected from the direction of the spotlight. Bitmap shadows have a softer edge and require less calculation time; however, they are also less accurate than ray-trace shadows. Using the ray trace option will create shadows with hard edges and will realistically render transparent materials. Note that ray tracing takes more memory and time to calculate than shadow maps.

To improve on the accuracy of the cast shadows in your scene, use the ray-tracing option. Begin by selecting the target spotlight with your mouse. Access the **MODIFY** command panel. In the command panel, scroll down to *Shadow Parameters*. Select **Use Ray-Traced Shadows**. Render the camera viewport again to examine the changes made to the cast shadows in the scene.

TIP ◀

*The clarity of cast shadows in a digital scene is the result of the intensity (brightness) and the parameter setting (ray trace) of individual spotlights.*

Ambient light is used to simulate general, low-level illumination. For most renderings, the default setting provided by 3D Studio VIZ is adequate. Manipulating the ambient setting will affect the entire scene; changing the hue will give an overall, uniform tint to the digital environment. The options for ambient light are found under the **RENDERING\Environment** pull-down menu. Located under *Atmosphere*, find a dark box labeled *Ambient Light*. Pick on the box to activate the Color Selector dialogue box. Adjust the color and render the camera scene again. Return *Ambient Light* to the default setting: R=10, G=10, B=10, H=0, S=0, V=10.

Finally, 3D Studio VIZ offers several shading modes. You can access these by right-clicking on a viewport title. A drop-down menu will list the following: *Smooth + Highlight*, *Faceted + Highlight*, and *Wireframe*. You have been using wireframe throughout this tutorial. Pick on **Smooth + Highlight**. This is a simple shading mode and will not display cast shadows or show true colors (similar to Gouraurd). Next pick on **Faceted + Highlight**. Another simple shading mode, it renders flat surfaces without textured materials and does not support cast shadows (Figure 5-15). Only full-color rendering (Phong or metal) will support a quality image containing realistic color, materials, highlights, and shadows. Therefore, final images should always be rendered using the rendering command.

▶ **TIP**

*In addition to omni and target spotlights, 3D Studio VIZ offers two other types of lights: free spotlights and directional lights. Free spotlights are used primarily with animation and are linked to a keyframe path. Directional lights cast a parallel beam of light and are therefore used frequently to simulate the sun.*

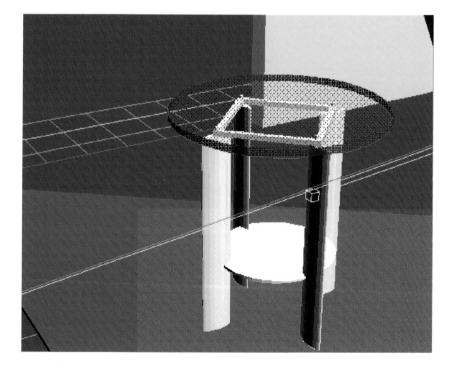

▶ Figure 5-15

Example of a table using a simple shading mode

## CHAPTER 5

## Summary

*Note that some rendering effects are controlled through the Material Editor, not through individual lighting features. For example, a mirrored or high-gloss surface is defined with reflectance maps, not the intensity of the light. Neon and similar objects, which glow from within, are created by defining the material's self-illuminating properties. Locating a light inside a cylindrical tube will not simulate a glowing material like neon. For more information about surface materials, see Chapter 4.*

Light is a dynamic factor in the natural and built environment. Because it's constantly moving and changing, light has traditionally been a challenge for the design community to simulate and study. However, digital rendering packages now provide a powerful tool that can quickly and accurately calculate projected light and shadow patterns within any existing or virtual space. This amount of valuable information at the designer's desktop stimulates visual thinking and guides important and costly design decisions. Although the computer has its strengths in calculating and rendering, it is the digital artist who is responsible for defining the character of each light source in the virtual environment.

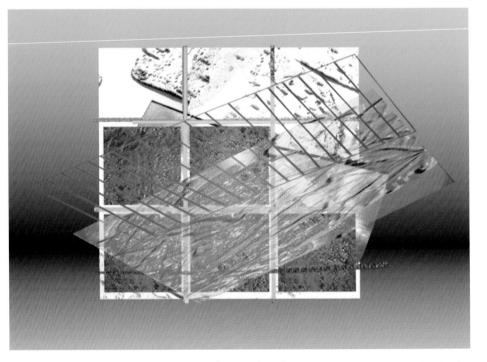

Sapsucker Woods Observatory, presentation and concept board          **Brian Davies**

*From the earliest examples of cave drawings, artists of one type or another have attempted to depict a sense of motion in their work. In doing so, the seed of animation was planted in the collective artistic subconscious; and it comes one step closer to fruition with each attempt to commit the captivating and often hypnotic quality of motion to canvas or clay. Today, a medium undreamed of by the ancient cave dwellers — the computer — is taking animation to a new level.*

> *While it is important to continue to develop verbal literacy, it is important to develop visual literacy as well. Graphic, video, and other modes of multimedia have great potential for conveying information and giving expression to ideas.*
>
> *- M. von Wodtke*

# Introduction

The idea of creating motion in art and design has been studied and analyzed by both designers and artists. Historically, artists have depicted moments in history through the use of drawings, tapestries, engravings, and photographs. These visual narratives created motion through the sequential order of the pictures. The 231-foot Bayeux tapestry, telling the story of the Norman Conquest of England in 1066, is an excellent example of the twelfth-century approach to an involved pictorial sequence (Hamilton, 1970). Sequential movement in graphics was utilized long before many people could read and write. It was a way for the viewers to understand history and pass it on to their descendants, thus making it an essential element for the perpetuation of cultures and historic events.

Sequential movement of a still image developed into animation, which first appeared in a rudimentary form in the mid-nineteenth century. On the Zoetrope, one of the first devices for animating still images, individual images were placed around the perimeter of a wheel. When the wheel was spun, the viewer looked through a fixed slot at the front of the wheel and saw, in quick succession, each image pass by. If the wheel was spun fast enough, the viewer's eye fused the still images together and saw the sequence as a moving image. The origin of traditional animation is inextricably linked to the development of motion picture technology. With people such as Eadweard Muybridge, Thomas Edison, and George Eastman hard at work laying the foundation for the film industry, other lesser-known figures were about to take the film pioneers' work in another direction. Animation would get its official start when, in 1906, a man named J. Stuart Blackton created the first animated film, called *Humorous Phases of Funny Faces* (Morrison, 1994).

For the next few years several people produced short animated films, but it was not until nine years later that traditional animation saw what is arguably its greatest advance. Around 1913, Earl Hurd developed cel (celluloid or cellulose) animation, the name by which traditional animation was known thereafter. In this technique, each character in the animation is drawn on a separate piece of transparent paper called a **cel**. These cels were made of either cellulose nitrate, used from the 1920s through the 1950s, or cellulose acetate, a much more stable material, which is still used today. After all the cels were drawn, a background was drawn on a separate piece of opaque paper. The characters were then placed over the background, and the whole thing was photographed. Each photograph then became one frame in the final animation sequence.

It was not until the late 1950s that people began to look to computers as the next logical step in the advancement of animation. Around the mid-1950s, an abstract filmmaker named John Whitney, Sr., began experimenting with analog computers to create art. His first attempt involved 17 Bodine motors, 8 Selsyns, 9 different gear units, and 5 ball integrators. Then in 1958 Whitney used an M-5 anti-aircraft gunsight computer to create animations by allowing the computer to control the movement of the artwork and camera. It was this system that Whitney used to create the title sequence for Alfred Hitchcock's *Vertigo* and in 1961 his own animation called *Catalog* (Morrison, 1994).

By the early 1970s, in addition to the 3D modeling research being done at New York Institute of Technology (NYIT), many people were working to develop what was, at the time, the more practical area of 2D animation. Shortly after leaving the University of Utah (UU), Ed Catmull joined the NYIT team and went to work to develop a system that would use a computer to generate the in-between frames of an animation. After a master animator had painted the most important segments of an animation called

**keyframes**, it was the task of apprentice animators to generate the frames in between the keyframes, a process known as **tweening**. The product of Catmull's research was a tool called Tween, which was capable of interpolating the in-between frames from one line drawing to another (Morrison, 1994).

Today, most of the 2D animation film is produced on computers. Although computer-generated 2D animation remains very popular, many companies, including Disney, have begun to integrate 3D animation into their 2D animation films.

Since the early 1990s the world of interior and architectural design has started to introduce computer animation through the 3D walk-through. Since then, 2D animation has been overlooked by many in the design fields in lieu of more sophisticated 3D animation programs. However, the use of 2D animation can enhance the effectiveness of design communication and presentation involving text, diagrams, charts, and other visual illustrations. It is also a very effective visualization tool for understanding complex constructions or composed forms. Also, the experience in 2D animation can be a foundation for studying more advanced design visualization.

# Concepts

Two-dimensional animation has been used in many fields and in a variety of ways. This chapter mainly addresses the use of 2D animation in design presentation.

## Using 2D Animation as a Design Tool for Idea Generation and Presentation

With the use of animation, ideas take on a more complex form, are more vivid, and often are easier for people to understand. Through 2D sample diagrams and elements in motion, the design idea and its explanation are more thorough. Also, with an animated presentation, an abstract idea can become more interesting and exciting. This is an excellent way to present design concepts and characters in an effective visual format. Not only does the animated presentation reveal the designer's strength of creativity, but also it shows the designer's commitment to technology and innovative ways to work with the client.

Another advantage of studying 2D animation is that the various features of most 2D pixel-oriented computer animation programs are more related to the manual approach to animation than to the 3D object-oriented computer animation. It is easier and more comfortable to learn 2D animation before 3D animation with the computer. When creating an animated presentation, designers should always consider themselves as information designers and design communicators rather than animation technicians.

## Sequence and Structure

We are continually aware of the sequencing basic to the way we perceive our world. We note a temporal sequencing and word sequencing, which are fundamental to the organization or structuring of information vital to our life experience (Hamilton, 1970). "Sequence heightens clarity of visual exposition and introduces the aspect of discovery. It helps us to discriminate on the extended scale of space and time - the levels of the very large, the very small, the very fast, the very slow. . . . It is a part of all the essential rhythms of nature - the measured passing of time, the beating of the pulse, and the act of breathing" (p. 48-49).

Sequencing refers to the information placed in the animation, as well as preparing the function and artistic viewing experience. To remember and understand a still image and an animation is very different. Even "modern scientists theorize that memory is a chemical constituent of the brain. This is a satisfactory psycho-physiological explanation, but it doesn't answer the mystery of our daily memory experience and explain what external stimuli control our patterns of recall" (Hamilton, 1970, p.138). After the contents of the animation have been organized in a structured pattern and presented in a distinct style with interesting images, it is only then that people will understand and remember what the presentation is about.

In general there are three different sequences of structure for creating a computer-based design presentation. First, the structure of animation reflects the process of the design; for example, the animation illustrates the design process - from introducing the design problem, researching the design, generating ideas, developing the design, documenting the material specifications, to constructing the actual design. This approach has clear linear sequence and is strongly tied to traditional design problem-solving processes, which are familiar to most people.

The second approach in sequencing the computer presentation starts with the animation showing the most impressive characteristic of the overall design. The viewer's attention is captivated from the very beginning of the presentation. In this approach not only the design itself requires creativity, but the sequencing of the whole animation. The challenge of this approach is to have clear and smooth transitions between each design phase.

The third sequence of the animation process is introduced in the next section.

## Multimedia Presentation

The first and second sequences of the animation structures do not involve interaction with multimedia. However, the third sequence of the animation process depends on the new concept of using the computer for the presentation.

By using computer technology in a presentation, with its flexibility and interactive features, the sequence is not only assigned by the designer, but the viewer participates in the organization process. The individual viewer, through different sequencing and combinations of the animation's contents, can search for his or her own answers. The presentation process becomes more flexible, interactive, and based on the individual preference of the viewer. The sequence can by customized.

*"You can engage many of your senses electronically - almost as if you were working with reality. Multimedia can help you draw channels of communication. ...In this way multimedia can help you draw upon more of your mental capacity when you learn, create, and communicate" (von Wodtke, 1993, p. 12).*

# CHAPTER 6

Two key principles distinguish the degree of interaction a viewer experiences when using multimedia: viewing, when a person is passively watching without really responding, and interacting, which involves actively viewing and doing what you visualize. Interacting is what children are doing when they play video games. When interacting with the presentation, the viewer not only uses left-brain or deductive modes of thought, but actively uses the right-brain or inductive modes of thought that are more visual and intuitive. This combined use of the left and right sides of the brain translates into creative mental energy, which actively interacts with the multimedia (von Wodtke, 1993). Numbers, text, graphics, models, images, and sounds are integrated within a design presentation in which the multimedia facilitates a situation and an environment and lets a viewer be a part of the communication process. It has stimulated the viewer's motivation to search for a better and more comprehensive understanding of the presentation.

In an interactive multimedia presentation, the several combinations which deliver information enable the viewer to be flexible in searching for the design solutions. The viewer may pick his or her own sequencing, which can be different from the designer's sequencing. So the structure of the presentation should be designed to accommodate as many combinations of paths as possible to suit the various viewer's needs. With the increased knowledge of digital media in design professions and education, the interactive method will soon become standard for design communication and presentation.

# Cognition

## Definition of a Simple Storyboard

A **storyboard** is a visual interpretation of the sequence of frames that you wish to create in your presentation, which can be in both manual and digital formats. It describes the process of your design and communicates ideas through visual images and notes. To define a storyboard, one simply works within boxes (or frames) to convey ideas. These boxes are laid out in a sequence to which they may be added or revised for your entire animation. The storyboard, then, becomes the framework for the actual animated presentation.

## The 2D Animation Illusion and Keyframe

Animation is the illusion of movement. This illusion of movement can be achieved by quickly displaying a series of images that show slight incremental changes in one of the depicted objects.

Human visual acuity is low enough that only 12 to 15 different pictures (or frames) need to be displayed per second to produce the illusion of movement. However, these low speeds make the movements appear jerky, so television or video typically displays 30 frames per second (fps), while film uses about 24 fps. This means that when animation is created for television, 30 separate pictures are flashed before your eyes every second. Your mind perceives the sequence of individual still images as fluid, continuous movement (Morrison, 1994).

In traditional animation the main artists usually only draw the frames that contain the key or main movements of the character or a space. To fill in the missing frames, assistant artists, called in-betweeners, draw the in-between frames. The in-betweeners do their drawing work on a light table, using transparent sheets of paper. As they draw each frame, they overlay the next page on top of it and then slightly vary the movement depicted in the new frame, so when the sequence is played back at a high speed, the movement appears natural. Because this process is time-consuming, many designers have not adopted this traditional animation as a format to animate their design. The computer solves the problem by following the keyframes, which are created by the designer; then it generates the in-between frames. For example, the designer only specifies the keyframes, such as looking at the building entrance, turning points, and looking up and around; then the computer makes all the transitional frames in between the major turning points.

## The 2D Animation Categories

According to computer graphics designer Mike Morrison (1994), 2D computer animation can be divided into four main categories: animated cels, optical effects, tweening or morphing, and color cycling.

TIP ◀

*In most other software, the cut, copy, and paste process is very similar to the process of creating a cel, as explained above.*

**Cels** (short for celluloids), are not frames, but they can become frames. Traditional cels are clear sheets of plastic upon which images are painted before being photographed for traditional animation. A **frame** is a single picture that you create on the screen. Each frame has one complete picture, and when the picture is projected fast enough, the frames appear to be in motion. It is a single frame that makes up a sequence of animated frames called an animation. In Autodesk's Animator Pro, and most animation software, the cel supports the capability to clip out a variety of sizes or portions of the screen image for pasting and other types of image editing. Cel files can be used as maps and backgrounds.

**Optical effects** include many manipulation tools, such as changing scale, moving position, rotation, and spinning. Cels and images can be used as optical effects to achieve a level of interest, especially at the beginning and end of each animated cel and image. For example, the title of the presentation can expand from miniscule to a prominent position on the screen. Also, the last image of the presentation can spin, reduce in size, and finally slowly fade out.

**Tweening** and **morphing** both reflect the transition process. "Tweening takes two different objects (on different frames) and creates the in-between frames needed to make a smooth transition between them. Morphing simply means that as the first object starts to transform itself into the shape of the second object, the computer slowly fades the first object out of the sequence" (Morrison, 1994). In design, we may use the morphing feature to visualize the transition from an abstract design diagram to a concrete floor plan.

"**Cycling** is a method of animation wherein you only use one frame or picture, while the computer cycles, or shifts, the colors in a predetermined pattern" (Morrison, 1994). This effect can add special color combinations and alternate lighting illusions to a presentation.

Besides good sequencing, the special effects in the animation are one element that designers can use to enrich their presentation and reflect their creativity while merging technology and the design content.

## Steps for Creating a 2D Animation

Most animation programs provide the tools and certain processes to create impressive and believable illusions in motion. After you create the storyboard and elements you want to animate, the 2D animation generally consists of three steps:

1. Create a series of frames.
2. Specify the illusion you want to create. In other words, decide what visual effect you want to achieve (i.e., an object that moves from place to place, changes size, or spins).
3. Render the sequence of frames. After you specify the setting, you need to give the command to let the computer render all the frames together. Some software programs do the rendering and save some time, but others do not.

The most efficient way to create a complex animation for design visualization is to create the whole animation separately and then link the separate animation together to make sophisticated presentation files. There are several advantages to this approach. First, this reduces the chance of losing all files. Second, it is easier to manage separate files. Third, this approach has the flexibility of putting the sequence in the whole animation. Each segment of the animation can be created by different programs, depending on the nature of its contents. As in the design process, each phase of the design has its own features so the entire animation should accommodate those individual features. In this chapter we study only the general concept for linking 2D animation files.

# Applications

## Learning to Create Cels in Animator Pro

In Animator Pro, from the CEL menu, select **Get**. The result is that the Home panel disappears, the menu bar changes into a status line, and crosshairs appear in the drawing area. Select the area of image that you want to capture in a cel by clicking at the upper corner of that image (this is the cel in a cel buffer). This sets the first corner of the cel. Move the cursor diagonally down toward the lower right corner of the selected image (the selected image is now enclosed in the box area). You have now created a cel (Figure 6-1). You may decide to copy that image somewhere else, in which case you could select **Paste** from the CEL menu. Then click inside the cel, and by moving the mouse, place the cel in another part of the frame by clicking on the desired point. Another option is to leave the cel in the cel buffer for future use. The cel buffer is an area reserved for memory, containing either part of an entire frame or part of an entire animation. In addition to the image data, the cel buffer contains information describing the position of its center, plus all palette information. You can store the contents of the cel buffer on a disk for repeated use. A cel can be moved, stretched, mirrored, rotated, or pasted onto one or more frames.

**Figure 6-1** ◀

Manual sketch
rendering

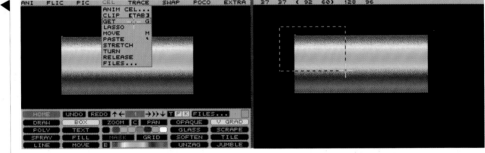

## Using Animator Pro to Create Animated Text

Let's begin with a quick look at the interface of Animator Pro. The top bar is a series of pull-down menus. After you select one of the menus, a panel appears with command options. The Home panel is the base for the program. On the left side of the panel, there are eight drawing tools. You can select more tools or modify the current tool by clicking on the right mouse button on one of the rectangles that leads you to the Tools panel. In the right portion of the Home panel, there are eight boxes that contain different editing features. By highlighting one of the rectangles and then clicking the right mouse button, proceed to the Ink panel. You can select different inks or modify the current ink setting (Figure 6-2). In the center of the Home panel are the frame control tools, zoom tools, and color palette tools. Selecting one of them takes you to its individual panel. For more details see the Animator Pro manual.

Now to create some animated text. From the Home panel, go to the ANI menu on the top of the screen and select **Tilting**. From the first column of commands, select Load Font (Figure 6-3). Select the desired font (the fonts will appear in the center box). Then adjust the Leading, Spacing, and Height options. Select Load (this will take you back to the Tilting panel). Now

▶ **TIP**

*Move the cursor outside of the panel, and click on the right mouse button. You can return to the Home panel.*

▶ **TIP**

*If the text never appears, check to make sure the ink is colored and not black ink, which is invisible on the blank screen.*

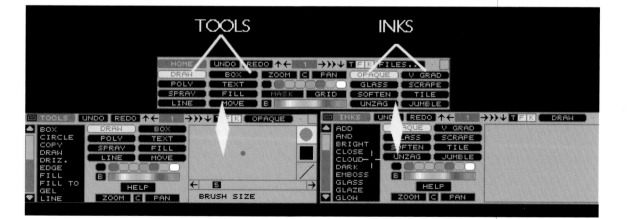

▶ **Figure 6-2**

Changing panels to perform modifications

**TIP** ◄

*On the Frames Icon (at the top center of the Home panel), click on the double arrows (>>) to play the animation. If you stopped the animation somewhere in the middle (the current frame number appears in the middle of the Frame Icons), you could easily rewind it to the first frame: On the Frame Icons, click on the up arrow (^). Frame 1 appears on screen, and its number appears in the Frame Icons.*

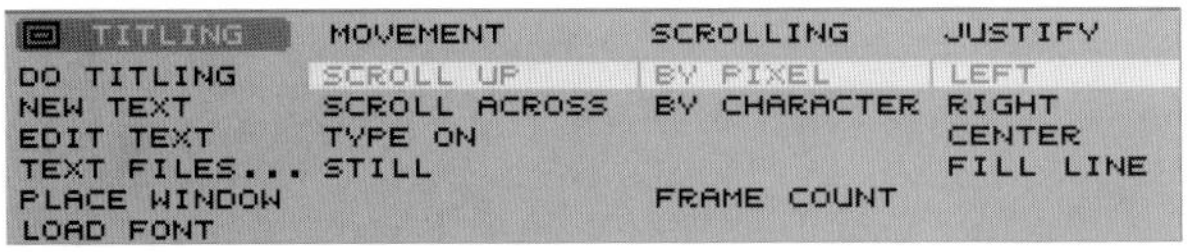

select **New Text**. With the crosshairs now seen on the screen, create a box by clicking in the upper corner and moving diagonally to the lower right. This will create the box in which to write your text.

Write your text. When you have finished, click on the right mouse button. The text will disappear, and the Tilting panel will reappear.

Now, from the other columns in the Tilting panel, select the desired animation effect (i.e., from the first column, *Movement*, select **Scroll Up**; from the second column, *Scrolling*, select **By Pixel**; and from the third column, *Justify*, select **Left**). Be sure to experiment with these different effects.

When you have finished, select **Do Tilting**, and the Time Select panel will appear. Here you want to create frames for the animation. To do so, right-click on the **Frames Icon** button (where the box with the shaded number 1 is located). This brings you to the Frames panel (Figure 6-4). In the Frames panel, right-click on the number 1 in the small box to the right of the down arrow. Where indicated, type in the number of frames desired for the animation (that is, 40). Then select **OK**. When you have finished, right-click on the black screen, which brings you back to the Time Select panel. Select **Preview** (this allows you to see what the finished animation will look like). If this is the desired effect and everything appears the way that you want it, select **Render**.

Right-click back to the Home panel to view the animation. Simply click on the double arrows to play the finished animation. Save as a flic file. To do so, under the **FLIC** menu on the top of the screen, select **Files**. On the Files panel, select **Save**. Choose the desired directory and name your file, and then click on **Save**.

**Figure 6-3** ◄

Modifying Titling panel

```
□ TITLING      MOVEMENT      SCROLLING     JUSTIFY
DO TITLING     SCROLL UP     BY PIXEL      LEFT
NEW TEXT       SCROLL ACROSS BY CHARACTER  RIGHT
EDIT TEXT      TYPE ON                     CENTER
TEXT FILES...  STILL                       FILL LINE
PLACE WINDOW                 FRAME COUNT
LOAD FONT
```

**Figure 6-4** ◄

Setting up number of frames for animation

```
FRAMES  ↑ ←[          1          ]→ ›› ↓  1 I  INSERT
SEGMENT  A B C D  MARKS  A B C D  x2 x3 x5  DELETE
←  1  →[                         ]← 1 → ⊟⊙⊟   1
PLAY SPEED ← 5                   →    TIME SELECT
```

## Creating a Presentation Opening

After you enter Animator Pro, reset the working environment to prepare for the new drawing. Go to the **FLIC\Reset**. Accept the standard default of 320 x 200. Now begin a simple animation. The first step is to create a background for the animation. To create the background, click on the square in the top right corner of the Home panel. This is the Current Color box. By clicking on the box you will proceed into the Palette panel. Click on **CLUSTER\Get Cluster** (Figure 6-5). You will select a color palette to use for the background.

The number corresponding to the color, highlighted by the cursor, is displayed on the top menu bar. Click on number **196** and click again to stop on **201**. These six colors will become your current B cluster. Right-click on the mouse outside the Palette panel to return to the Home panel. Click on the **Vgrad** box on the right side of the Home panel. Go to **PIC\Apply Ink**. The color is applied to the background in a vertical gradation (Figure 6-6). Save this file as a "gif" file for later use by clicking on **PIC\Files\Save**. Name your file **Background** and save it to the appropriate destination. Then click on **Save**.

In order for the background to be present throughout the whole animation, you must render it to become an animation file. To do this, move the cursor on the center top of the frame control box in the Home panel (dark shaded box with 1 on top) and right-click, which leads you to the Frames panel. Move the cursor to the small rectangular box with the number 1 in it, and right-click, which leads you to a box where you modify the number of frames. Type in **40**, and then click on **OK**. Your animation file is now 40 frames long. Right-click outside the frame panel to return to the Home panel.

> ▶ **TIP**
>
> *Move the cursor outside the Home panel and right-click to see the full screen without any panels. Right-click again to return to the panels.*

▶ **Figure 6-5**
Creating a new cluster

▶ **Figure 6-6**
Background image

Go to **ANI\Optics**. Click on **Use** without changing the spin, size, or view factors. Click on **Render** to make the image rendered to all 40 frames. Click on **Presets\Quit Optics** to return to the main menu. Click on **FLIC\Files\Save**. Name the file background. This time it will be saved as a flic file, which is an animation file.

Now you begin to create the letters, and then you animate them. Click on **FLIC\Reset**, and then select the orange color from the color box in the minipalette in the center portion of the Home panel. Highlight the **Text** rectangle, right-click on **Text**, and then left-click on **Font**. Select **SERBI 14**. Then click on **Load** and return to the Home panel by clicking on the right mouse button outside the Tools panel.

Using the Text tool, click in the upper left corner of the screen and drag the cursor to the right side of the screen to form a rectangle about 2 inches tall. Then type CBRF. Inside the rectangle, click on the left button to drag the word to the upper center of the screen. Then left-click to leave it in the new position or right-click to set it in the new position (Figure 6-7). Select **PIC\File\Save**. Name the file **Letters.gif**. This way you can use each letter individually to put them in motion.

Select a black color from the color minipalette. Using the box command, draw a black box to cover the letters BRF. This way we will only animate the letter C. Select **CEL\Clip**. After you see the white-dashed box around the C, select **PIC\Clear**. Click on **File\Load**. Load background.flc, which you just created.

**Figure 6-7** ◀
Creating
main title

Now you create the motion by selecting **ANI\Optics**. This will take you to the Optics window. Select **Element\Cel** to make sure the element of motion is just the cel and not the entire frame. Select **Move** from the Optics panel. In the direction bar box, move the slider to the left to **−162** (Figure 6-8). Then click on **View**. A white dashed line should show the motion of the letter C.  If the effect is desired, click on **Use,** which leads you to the Time Select  panel. Select **Reverse** and then **Preview**. After previewing, select **Render**. Then click on the double arrow to play the animation and select **Presets\Quit Optics** to return to the Home panel. Select **FLIC\Files\Save**. Name the file **Letter C** and save as a flic file.

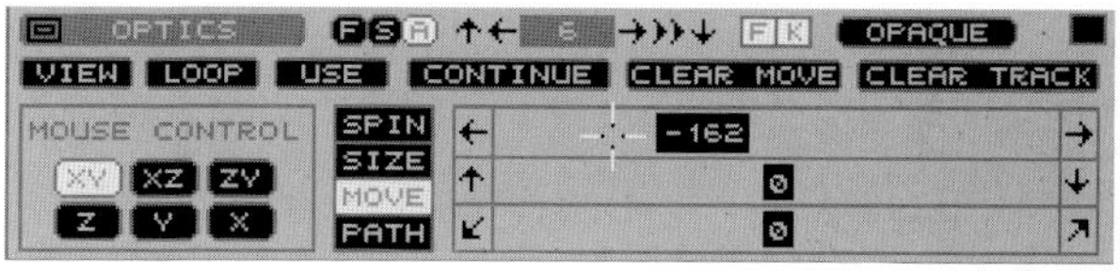

Now animate the second letter B. Return to the first frame of the **Background.flic** file by clicking on the up arrow in the middle of the Home panel. Click on **PIC\File\Load**

▶ **Figure 6-8**

Movement settings

and load the file **Letters.gif**. Select black from the minipalette and opaque from the right side of the Home panel. Select the Box tool and cover all letters except for B. Click on **CEL\Clip**. After the white box disappears, click on **PIC\Clear**. Click on **ANI\Optics**. Make sure Cel is selected in the Elements menu. Click on **Clear track** on the right side of the Optics panel to clear all of the previous settings. Click on **Move** and move the arrow up to **−162**. Click on **Use** and make sure **Reverse** is selected. Click on **Render**. Then click on **Presets\Quit Optics.**

Next animate the letter R.  Make sure you return to the first frame and then follow the same process used for the letter B.  However, after you select **Clear track**, move the down arrow to **162**.

Use the same procedure to animate the letter F. This time after you select Clear track, move the right arrow to **162**. Select **Presets\Quit Optics**.

Before you save, delete the first frame by moving your cursor on the frame portion of the Home panel and then right-clicking. In the Frame panel, make sure you are on the first frame and then hit **Delete** on the far right side of the frame panel. Make sure you save the final result as **CBRF1.flc**. Also save the last frame of the flic file as **CBRF1.gif**.

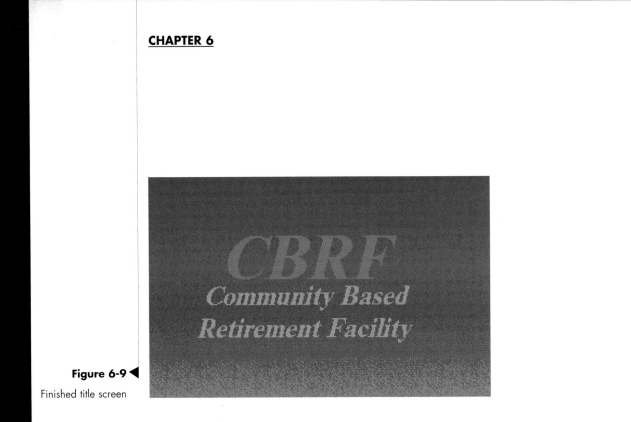

**Figure 6-9** ◄

Finished title screen

Now you have finished the first part of the animation and can proceed to the next part. Begin by clicking on **FLIC\Reset**. Highlight the **Text** rectangle, and then click on **Text\Font**. Select the font **SERBIO6** and then click on **Load**. Right-click to return to the Home panel.

Select the light blue color. Using **Text,** create a large rectangle and type in the words **Community-Based** on the first line and hit [Return]. Then type **Retirement Facility** on the second line inside the box. Click on **CEL\Clip**. Click on **PIC\Clear**.

Load the last frame of the previous flic file and use it as the background for the current animation. Click on **PIC\Files\Load**. Load the file **CBRF1.gif**. Click on **CEL\Move**. Using the left mouse button, move the text under the word CBRF (Figure 6-9). Increase the number of frames to 40. Click on **ANI\Optics**. Click on **Elements\Cel**. Click on **Size** in the Optics panel, and move the slider from 100 to 0 in the Reduce slide bar. Click on **Use**, which takes you to the Time Select panel. Highlight **Reverse** and click on **Render**. The words in blue should move out from the center of the screen and increase in size. The letters CBRF should remain in place. Click on **Presets\Quit Optics**. Save as a flic file and name it **CBRF2.flc**.

Click on **FLIC\Reset** to start a new file. Select **FLIC\Files\Load**. Load **background.flc**. Make sure you move to the first frame. Click on **PIC\Clear** to return the preset black background.

Select **Text\Font\SERBI08\Load**. Select a light blue color from the cluster bar in the Home panel. Using the Text tool, create a rectangle, starting in the upper left corner of the screen and dragging the cursor to the lower right corner of the screen. Then click on the mouse button. Type in the text **Designed By**. Select **CEL\Get** and select the text. Select **PIC\Clear** and then **ANI\Optics** to proceed to the Optics panel. Select **Element\Cel**. Click on **Size**, and move the Reduce slide bar from 100 to 0. Click on **Use**. In the Time Select panel, highlight **Reverse** and click on **Preview**. The text should appear in the middle of the screen, changing from small to large. If you like the result, click on **Render**. Then click on **Presets\Quit Optics** to go back to the Home panel.

Move to the first frame. Using the **Text** tool, type in your name. Right-click on the mouse button to set on the screen. Select **CEL\Get** and select your name. Move to the last frame of this animation; this gives you the previous image of the words Designed by, which will enable you to move the new text – your name – to the proper position on the screen. Select **CEL\Move**. Using the left mouse button, move the text underneath the words Designed by. When it is in the correct position, left-click to set it on the screen.

Select **PIC\Clear** and then **ANI\Optics**. From the Optics panel select **Move**, and move the down arrow slide bar to **150**. Also click on **Spin\Turns**. Highlight 1\360 and move the left arrow slide bar to –700. Click on **Use**. Highlight **Reverse** and click on **Preview**. Your name should spin up from the bottom of the screen and end just below the words Designed by. Click on **Render**. Select **Presets\Quit Optics**. Return to the first frame of the animation, and delete the first frame. Select **FLIC\Files\Save**. Name it **CBRF3.flc**.

Now link the individual animations together. Before this, you must plan what files go first, second, and so on to create the whole animation. Load the file CBRF1.flc, and then select **FLIC\Join**. Then from the Load Flic 2 to Merge with CBRF1.flc panel, select your second file CBRF2.flc to merge with CBRF1.flc. Click on **Load**. In the Join panel there are several options: Cut, Custom, Dissolve, and Boxilate. Highlight **Dissolve** (Figure 6-10). Click on **Render**, and then play the merged animation.

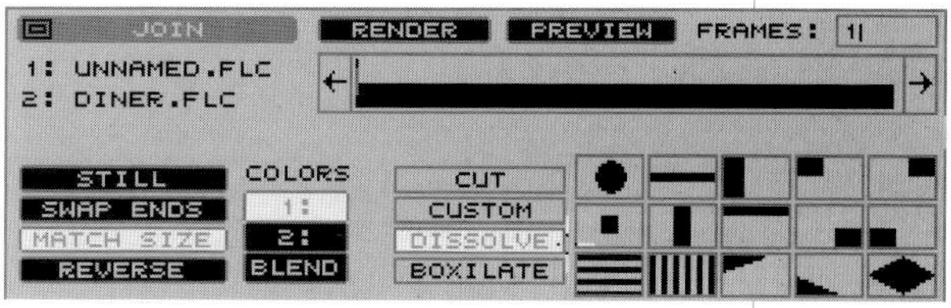

▶ **Figure 6-10**

Join settings

**NOTE** ◄

*If you want to see a
similar file created
by Nicole Sharp,
load FINAL.FLC
on the CD.*

Select **FLIC\\Join** again, and then select **CBRF3** and **Load**. In the Join panel, highlight **Dissolve**. Click on **Render**. Then click on the double arrow to play the whole animation, and save as **Final.flc**.

## Interactive Presentation

This section is only a general process for one of many ways to create an interactive presentation. This tutorial uses AutoCAD to create a 3D model; then it imports the model into 3D Studio R4 or 3DS MAX for material and lighting study, as well as creates a 3D walk-through. Also, from the AutoCAD model, export several images into Photoshop for image manipulation, such as floor plans, elevations, or perspectives. Those images can be used for opening or transitional images. Use Animator Pro to create some 2D effects for transitional use, and use Photoshop for scanning images and manipulating images to include in the presentation. A scanner may also be used to generate some images and in the presentation as reference or background images.

**NOTE** ◄

*The files named
"Rita.exe" and
"Mindy.exe" in the
subdirectory folder
"Rita" or "Mindy"
in CH6 on the
attached CD are
examples of
simple interactive
presentations.*

When all of the project's sections are finished, it is time to use Director to link all of them together. First, you need to convert all the animation files into a "Quick-time movie." From the Director program, import all the files which you have created so that you can manipulate them easily and put them in a correct sequence in the presentation. To do this, you need to create transitional pages which allow the viewer to look at the presentation interactively. On the transitional pages there should be text to tell the viewer the contents and icons (hot buttons) for the viewer to click on for viewing different sections of the presentation.

Once all the transition pages are created, insert all the separate files (different parts of the project) in a sequential order. Use the script portion of Director to indicate which sequences of its function. The script tells the computer which part of the project to go to when a certain button is clicked. After all the sections are in a correct sequence, test several times before saving the complete presentation file.

## Summary

This tutorial has shown how to create a simple animated presentation using some of the basic tools in Animator Pro. It is important to remember that Animator Pro contains many sophisticated tools, such as 2D morphing, image filters, and many others, which, with patience and practice, can be harnessed to create truly stunning presentations. In much the same way as traditional hand-drawn animation has fascinated and excited people for almost a hundred years, 2D animation has the potential to do the same by clarifying complex ideas while dramatically enhancing their visual presentation.

Flad & Associates Lobby

*In the whirlwind of excitement that surrounds new visualization technology, it is sometimes easy to forget that the technology is not an end unto itself, but rather a means by which to enhance our understanding of the world around us. It is essential to the success of the creation process that we, as designers and architects, understand not only our perception of the environment within which we exist, but also the perception of others who share that environment.*

*The sketch, perspective, or rendering, showing a space in more or less realistic fashion, becomes the key document to explain a design proposal*
*- J. Pile*

# Introduction

In the design profession, renderings may be described as black and white or full-color representations of a proposed design. Renderings may be small or large, loosely or precisely drawn to scale (Leach, 1978).

Rendering, as a major part of the architectural drawing, has reflected the development of architectural and interior design. In the early development of architectural design, rendering seemed lifeless; it lacked imagination and communication. There was no depth of perception nor was there a sense of the totality of the designer's idea. The return of richness and romanticism to rendering reminds us of the roots of an art that began to reach maturity in the Renaissance. Gradually, its practitioners became adept at drawing images as seen by the human eye, where distant objects appear increasingly smaller and taper to a vanishing point on the horizon (Gapp, 1988).

By the early twentieth century, architects were expressing a whole range of stylistic methods inspired by photography and printed documents. But this wasn't enough, for architects needed methods to represent their ideas in a more realistic fashion. Realistic drawing by architects finally became a major professional activity only with the arrival of formal architectural education... [Rendering] drawings thus came to have a purpose beyond merely giving information to a contractor; they must come as close as possible to the reality of an actual building.

With the coming of Modernism in the 1920s and 1930s, some architects thought that realistic drawing was inadequate to represent their design styles. The renderings became less emphasized in architectural education while sternly technical working drawings that laymen like to call 'blue-prints' were used instead to communicate the design idea with the contractors (Pile, 1967, p. 9).

In the Modernist movement, several pioneers have also expanded the meaning and dimensions of rendering. Le Corbusier's drawings depend mostly on line to define form, making little attempt to suggest realistic effects of light and atmosphere. Mies Van der Rohe's drawing is well suited to conveying the spirit of his work, while not being realistic drawings in the usual sense (Pile, 1967). Frank Lloyd Wright was a master draftsman, and his drawing reflected his strong interest in expressing design on paper. He used various types of papers, pens, and pencils to render objects with a broad range of realistic approaches from simple shades and shadows to complete photographically realistic images. His drawings have merged together engineering accuracy, architectural creativity, and artistic expression.

When Postmodernism developed in the1970s, it expanded the meaning of architectural rendering. "It drew on forms from the past and played a major role in the revival of elaborate architectural drawing as a fine art, a means of inspiration, and a cerebral exercise" (Gapp, 1988, p. 20).

The function of architectural and interior design rendering has expanded in many directions. Some of the current renderings are strong, romantic, whimsical, and even polemical. Others are simply intended as theoretical statements about design. The book *Postmodern Visions: Drawings, Paintings, and Models by Contemporary Architects*, edited by Heinrich Klotz (1985), carefully documents the variety and type of renderings in the Postmodern age. Examples of the phenomenal renderings of the era include Raimund Abraham, Michael Graves, Helmut Jahn, Ettore Sottsass, Aldofo Natalini, etc.

Coincidentally with the Postmodern age, computer technology revolutionized rendering. Technology opened new opportunities for applying rendering in design from design simulations to building materials and lighting studies. The achievements led to the ultimate viability of this process: the idea of applying computer imaging and rendering techniques to environmental simulations, which is a rela-

*"Centuries ago, civilization crossed a threshold of literacy. Many people gained access to the tools needed to work creatively on traditional media, such as paper. As a result, creativity flourished and became manifested in a period that came to be known as the Renaissance. . . . Today, civilization is crossing yet another threshold - computer literacy. Individuals once again have access to new tools for creativity"* (von Wodtke, 1993, p. 132).

tively new concept. However, it can be traced to the early work of many of the computer graphics pioneers.

The first major advancement in the area of computer imaging came in 1961 when, while working at the Massachusetts Institute of Technology, Ivan Sutherland invented the first interactive drawing program, called Sketchpad. The program allowed users to draw simple shapes on a computer screen by using a light pen. Once the shapes were drawn, they could be saved and recalled later. Around the middle 1970s, Alvy Ray Smith made the move from Xerox to join Ed Catmull at New York Institute of Technology. Shortly thereafter, Smith developed the first full-color (24-bit) paint program (Morrison, 1994).

With computer imaging techniques well in hand by the early 1980s, several people at various institutions turned their attention to the advancement of computer rendering techniques. In order for a computer to render an object, scene, or animation, the computer must first have a model through which to understand the interactions among light, materials, objects, and motion. This type of model is what comprises a renderer, and it is differences in the model that distinguish one renderer from another.

In the early days of 3D modeling, each company or university had its own unique renderer, as was the custom with all software in those days. It was not until 1980 that the first work was done on what would later become one of only a handful of standard renderers. In that year, Turner Whitted published a paper on a new method for rendering highly reflective surfaces. The technique involved the tracing of a light source from its origin to an object, and then depending on the surface quality of the object, the light would bounce off the object and continue or would be absorbed. The technique later became known as **ray tracing** (Morrison, 1994).

One year later in 1981, a veteran programmer from Boeing Aircraft, Loren Carpenter, joined Lucasfilm. With numerous rendering algorithms already under his belt, Carpenter set out to write the first renderer for Lucasfilm. It is a safe assumption that at the time Carpenter had no idea that the renderer he created, called REYES (Render Everything You Ever Saw), would eventually become one of the most influential and powerful renderers even to this day. The REYES renderer eventually became Renderman, which now belongs to Pixar. In 1991 it was used by the company, in conjunction with Disney, to produce the first feature-length 3D animated film, called *Toy Story*. The next piece of the rendering puzzle fell into place when, in 1984, several people at Cornell University, including Cindy Goral and Don Greenberg, published a paper called "Modeling the Interaction of Light between Diffuse Surfaces." The technique described in the paper was based on the theory that the dispersion of light within an environment could be described to a computer in much the same way as heat dispersion, an already existing formula. This type of rendering model became known as **radiosity**, and it has since virtually closed the gap between lighting in reality and computer-simulated lighting (Morrison, 1994).

# Concepts

## Studying the Use of Computer-Generated Rendering as a Design Tool

In *Technics of Interior Design Rendering and Presentation*, Sid DelMar Leach said, "Renderings should be as exact as possible. Color, texture, material presentation, mass, detail, and related surroundings are all elements contained in this type of artistic representation, and each must be as representative as possible" (1978, p. 5). Using conventional approaches, rendering was often divided into two categories: sketch rendering and formal rendering. **Manual sketch rendering** is used most often to generate ideas and provide communication in the early design stage. The amount of information obtained from a sketch rendering is limited (Figure 7-1). **Formal manual rendering** portrays a greater sense of a space closer to the "final finished" project, and often the image is intended as a marketing tool (Figure 7-2). In the manual rendering process, every designer's vision and understanding of certain environmental conditions are different. His or her ability for repeating the condition is also different; therefore, the outcome images often are different. The image is usually more individualized and expressed more intensely. Formal rendering has long been viewed as the last stage in the design process.

In contrast with computer rendering, the flexible nature and the ability to quickly generate alternative solutions create the potential to expand the use of renderings in the design process. But the creation of a computer model and initial to learn the software can take time and the image sometimes has less individuality. **Computer rendering** is the process of using the computer to interpret the assigned materials, lighting, camera view, shading, etc., added to a modeled space or object, and the computer displays the result (Figure 7-3).

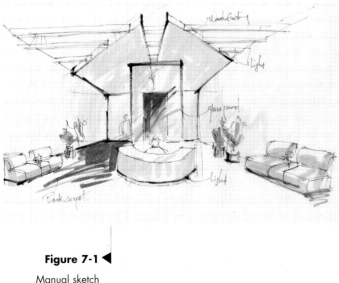

**Figure 7-1** ◀

Manual sketch rendering

Rendering is often a process of trial and experimentation with materials and settings until you achieve the desired effect. The ability to quickly experiment with multiple ideas makes the digital medium a very flexible tool for idea generation, communication, presentation, and evaluation of your design solu-

▶ **Figure 7-2**

Formal manual rendering

tion. For example, if you were designing a restaurant environment and wished to represent numerous combinations of tablecloths, plates, lighting, etc., it would be extremely time-consuming to produce all of the variations manually.

It is important to be aware of what each medium will do for different design processes. The discovery of a new medium is meant to provide additional choices and possibilities for improving the quality of the design rather than replacing one medium with others. The reinforcement of the strengths of each medium and the search for the best place to utilize them in the design process will continually challenge us to integrate digital technology in the design process.

▶ **Figure 7-3**

Computer rendering

## Exploring How Special Environmental Conditions Affect Our Perception of a Given Interior Space

The reason for creating a still-image rendering plays an important role in the current use of computer rendering in design. What follows are several alternative objectives for rendering and the settings that accomplish the goal of the rendering.

In general, most manual renderings are generated for the purpose of showing how certain design elements, such as materials and lighting, will look in a designed space. The goal is often to gain a visual image of how a space will appear aesthetically before it actually exists. The visual image of the rendering can be generated to give aesthetic information to a designer, a client, or both.

The digital medium has provided an opportunity to expand the use of rendering in design. Computer renderings not only generate images to compare alternative design solutions, but also provide information on how a space will appear under various environmental conditions.

To produce a believable or convincing simulation rendering, it is necessary to go beyond simply including basic lighting and materials. You must add a "real-life" environment or atmosphere. By adding some of the aforementioned elements to the image, not only do we have a much more convincing image, but also we can gain valuable information by examining the effect of such things as smoke or candlelight on a design. This visual information can often guard against costly renovations or dangerous situations. In fact, we can use rendering as a tool for studying how a given design is affected by special conditions such as power failure, fire, smoke, aging vision, or a child's view of the space.

By taking advantage of computer imaging and rendering techniques, designers are now able to visualize and simulate many different interior conditions not possible with manual techniques. With today's technology, the question is not how realistic the image can be, but what is the real purpose of the rendering. Is the purpose of the image to experiment with various materials, to try different lighting, or to see how the design might be viewed under certain conditions? Using the computer to focus on environmental conditions and special populations improves the designer's ability to make informed decisions throughout the design process. The Applications section in this chapter will cover several possible applications of imaging and rendering in the design process.

## Expanding the Experience of the Combination of Paint and Object-Oriented Programs

In general, there are two classifications of software which can generate 2D rendering: the 2D paint program and the 3D object-oriented program. Designs rendered using a **2D paint program** are based on pixels in a grid. The individual dots or pixels of color combine to form an image on the computer screen. The computer displays the pixels in the arrangement as they are drawn, and editing is done of the individual pixels. For example, if we draw a line in a 2D paint program, it is represented on the computer screen as a series of dots, one next to the other. If we then wish to change or edit that line, we must deal with each individual pixel as a separate entity. A paint program has a wide range of editing tools for manipulation of the image. It allows you to change or edit a portion of an image, and the assemblage of a composite image can be drawn through independent layering. However, an entire object cannot be manipulated as such, making rearranging and moving images very difficult. This is where **object-oriented software** can be beneficial. In an **object-oriented program**, the pieces in a rendering are created as objects and are recognized as objects by the computer for display and editing. For example, when you draw a chair, the entire chair can be moved or altered. The idea behind an object-oriented program is that the data is combined and contained by an object.

In some cases, the best approach to creating a still rendering is to use a combination of 2D and 3D software. For example, if your final rendering will be part of an advertisement for a chair, you might create the chair itself in a 3D program and then use a 2D paint program to make a composite of the finished chair with a picture of a living room as the background; then textual information can be added.

# Cognition

The computer is built and structured as a multipurpose tool for many different fields. Therefore, it is necessary to use a great deal of creative energy to tailor the computer for a specific purpose, which in our case is design visualization. Due to the general nature of the available tools, we must creatively apply the existing tools to expand our use of computer rendering. For example, there is no specific tool for simulating aging vision, but by creatively combining several more general tools, we can achieve that specific effect.

## Rendering Complex Lighting Effects

To produce accurate lighting effects in a computer rendering, three different methods may be employed. For the most basic types of lighting situations, highlights and shadows can be produced by using **shadow mapping**. This is the most basic type of lighting calculation. Although the shadows produced by this method have realistically soft edges, the placement of the shadows is not remarkably accurate, nor do they account for color cast.

The second method of lighting calculation is called **ray tracing**. In this method, the computer traces the path of a particular light source, thereby placing very accurate shadows. Although these types of shadows can cast color and are very accurate, they also have very hard edges, making them somewhat unconvincing. Furthermore, the process of ray tracing ends after the first time a light source encounters an object.

The resulting solution does not account for ambient light (diffuse interflections). For this type of lighting, it is necessary to use the final method of light calculation, known as **radiosity**. In this method, a very complex algorithm is used to determine the effect of various light sources on a scene. Due to the complexity of the radiosity algorithm, a great deal of computer resources are required to produce a realistic effect.

To determine lighting effects, the computer first divides all the surfaces in a scene into meshes. The size and characteristics of each square of a mesh are predetermined by the user. The computer then traces the path of each light source in the scene from its origin to the first surface that blocks its path. The computer determines to what degree the light is absorbed or reflected by the surface. Unlike ray tracing, the process is continued until all the light energy in the scene has been absorbed. The result is an extremely realistic rendering, complete with accurate soft shadows and correct ambient lighting.

To address the time and resource-consuming nature of a fully calculated solution, a method known as **progressive refinement radiosity** is used. This method uses the same technique as described above except that the solution is constantly updated, allowing the user to stop the calculation at any time. Unfortunately, radiosity, unlike ray tracing, does not account for specular reflections or transparency effects. It is therefore important to remember that in rendering, there is no one comprehensive solution to the creation of accurate lighting. It is possible, however, to employ a combination of methods to achieve the desired result.

## Rendering for Aging Vision

As we grow older, our eyes adjust and change the way that we see the world. An 80 year-old person will get a different impression than a 20 year-old person will get from the same space. No one can say exactly what difference will exist since every individual ages differently. But some general characteristics have been identified and can be adjusted for improved visual effects in a computer rendering.

The lens of the aging eye gradually yellows and clouds and may become less flexible. Because of this, older individuals require more light to see. Rendition of colors is affected by the yellowing, and the clouding takes away the perception of depth. The computer can be adjusted by lowering the light levels and by adding an atmosphere of yellow-tinted fog to the space, which will wash out some of the colors and will haze over the depth and three-dimensionality in the environment.

In 3D programs, **standard fog** is a 2D image overlaid onto the 3D environment, resulting in the appearance of fog over the entire image. **Layered fog**, like standard fog, is also a 2D effect. In this case, the fog appears as cloud cover or ground fog. **Volume fog** is a true 3D effect, which can generate anything from drifting clouds to wispy ground fog, all within the 3D environment. Additionally, to simulate the effect of blurring on elderly vision, 2D post-production software (Photoshop, etc.) can be used. By applying a "blur" filter effect to the final rendering, the desired effect may be achieved.

## Rendering a Smoky Environment

To add a haze of smoke, begin by filling the environment with a thin gray volumetric fog (3D fog). Next, layered fog can be added near the ceiling to simulate the natural collection of smoke at the top of a room.

## Rendering a Power Failure

A power failure is another environmental condition that can be represented in a computer rendering. To generate the image of a power failure, first turn off any representation of electric light sources in the space. Next, adjust any nonelectrical fixtures, such as exit signs, and adjust for light coming in the windows. The restaurant space that we rendered had self-illuminating energy storage exit signs above the exit doorways added to the space. Simulate light coming in the windows by creating directional lights and aiming them toward the window openings. The amount and adjustment of the light should reflect a given time of day and direction of light. Experiment with the illusion of light and adjust for different still-image scenes. It is impossible to adjust for all possible light conditions, but rendering a few will give valuable information to the designer (Figures 7-4 and 7-5). There is some advanced lighting simulation software now available that can create more scientific simulations.

**Figure 7-4** ◀
Power failure
simulation I

▶ **Figure 7-5**
Power failure
simulation II

## Rendering Sunrise and Sunset

When creating a computer rendering, sometimes it is necessary to represent time-dependent outdoor conditions. It is quite common to consider the time of day that an environment is most heavily used when making decisions about color and other design elements. For example, if the main entrance to a building is going to be used most often during sunrise, the choice of exterior finish has to be complementary to the often brilliant colors of sunrise. Similarly, if that building is located in an area prone to morning ground fog, walkways and obstacles have to be marked and positioned accordingly. By using a combination of colored lighting effects and computer-generated ground fog, a very accurate rendition can be produced of a typical sunrise in a given location.

## Rendering Fire

The smoky filtering and power failure can be combined with computer-generated flames to simulate an environment which is on fire. You can study the relationship between the fire and the visibility of the exit signs by using a combination of computer-generated flames and special colored lighting effects.

# Applications

## Understanding Some Features in the Computer Rendering Process

The images that follow are of the table modeled in 3D Studio R4, rendered to show some of the alternatives available with 3D Studio R4 described above. By studying the first four images, the concept of how changing the shading limit, to change the resulting rendering should be clear.

**TIP◄**

*Before beginning this tutorial, become familiar with the definitions and concepts specific to 3D Studio R4 and 3D STUDIO MAX. In addition to reviewing the definitions provided in the glossary of this book, take a moment to examine the definitions and basic concepts contained in the 3D Studio R4 and 3D STUDIO MAX manual.*

Figure 7-6, part A, is rendered with the shading limit set to **Flat**. This is the quickest rendering to complete but should only be used for test renderings or renderings where realistic images are not necessary. The materials are set to the object faces without smoothing between the faces. The result is a faceted surface. There is also no gradation in lighting in flat shading, resulting in a sharp, light-dark line being the only indication of light change.

Figure 7-6, part B, is rendered with the shading limit set to **Gouraud**. Gouraud rendering takes a little bit longer to complete than flat rendering; however, the result is somewhat smoother. The computer interpolates the colors between the faces at the adjoining vertices, giving the materials smoother transitions. This can be seen best by comparing the metal section of the legs in the flat and the Gouraud renderings. The Gouraud shading still limits the capability for realism of many of the materials and is seldom the desired setting for a final rendering.

Figure 7-6, part C, is rendered with the shading limit set to **Phong**. Phong shading interpolates the color between each pixel, as opposed to only at the vertices such as in Gouraud shading. The result is a realistic and smooth image. Many materials are Phong-shaded materials, so choosing this as the limit changes only a few materials, particularly metals. Phong shading is used in final renderings when metals or other metal-shaded materials do not play a large role in the scene.

Figure 7-6, part D, is rendered with the shading limit set to **Metal**. Metal shading interpolates the color the same way as Phong shading does. The difference with metal shading is seen in the specular highlights. Examine the difference between the metal section of the table legs. When metals are important in a scene for a final rendering, always set the limit to metal.

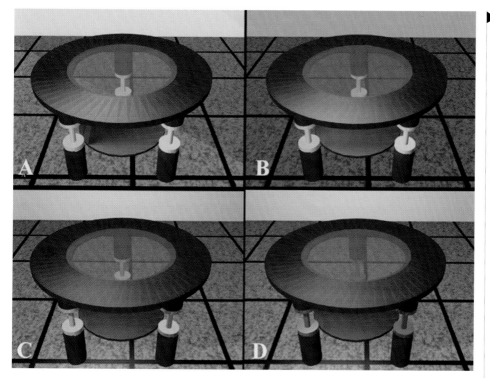

▶ **Figure 7-6**

Rendering shading

options

The next four renderings have fog added to the image scene. They are all identical TIF files with the shading limit set to Phong. The fog commands are located in the Rendering, Setup, and Atmosphere menus. When fog is added to a scene, there are two main options to consider. One is the color of the resulting fog, and the other is the amount and placement of the fog. The color is changed by modifying the RGB and HLS sliders. The amount and placement of the fog depends upon whether the atmosphere is added as fog, distance cuing, or layered fog, and how each of these selections is controlled.

▶ **TIP**

*The shading limit is
changed in the
Render Still-Image
dialogue box.*

Figure 7-7, part A, and Figure 7-7, part B, both contain the fog atmosphere. The fog atmosphere is set relative to the camera view of the scene. Because of this, the amount of fog near to and far from the camera can be adjusted. Part A is rendered with white fog of 10 percent near and 100 percent far. Part B has 40 percent near and 100 percent far. The difference is evident in the clarity of the object close to the camera viewpoint. Fog will become important later when we render a scene as aging eyes would view the environment.

**TIP ◄**

*The image rendered in 320 x 200 resolution only takes one fourth of the screen on the 640 x 480 VGA setting, but low resolution has the advantage of quick rendering for the testing purpose.*

Distance cuing has the same affect in a scene as black fog  All the colors are faded to black, and the amount of the fading can be adjusted relative to the camera near and far, as with the fog addition. The distance cuing emphasizes the depth of an image. It creates a dramatic effect in a large space and when the foreground of an environment needs emphasis.

Figure 7-7, part C, and Figure 7-7, part D, add layered fog to the scene. Layered fog is different from the other atmosphere options since the fog is not added to the scene relative to the camera but is fixed in place.  Changing the camera view does not alter the placement of the fog.  Because of this, instead of adjusting the amount near and far, the amount of fog can be adjusted in the top and bottom of the scene. Part C is rendered with 50 percent fog at the top of the scene and 20 percent at the bottom; (Figure 7-8) part D of is rendered with 50 percent fog at the top and 10 percent at the bottom. The color has also been changed to a light purple. The fog surrounds the camera, and because of this, layered fog will become important to creating the effect of a smoky environment.

▶ **Figure 7-7**

Fogging options

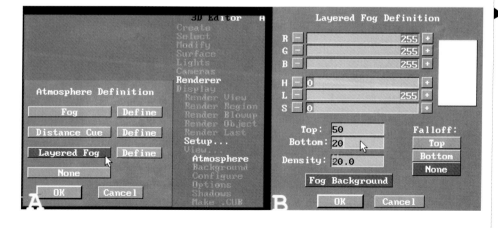

▶ **Figure 7-8**

Setting fog options

The following four images demonstrate the use of background in a rendering. To complete the images, the walls and the floor surrounding the table in the other renderings were deleted. Given the Render\Setup\Background commands, the computer will generate the background for an object.

Figure 7-9, part A, is an example of rendering with a solid background. Solid backgrounds are often used when all the focus and emphasis need to be on a particular object. Click on **Render\Setup\Background**, and then highlight the Solid Color bar on the Background Method panel. Click on the long black bar, and you will get the Define Solid Color panel, which allows you to change the background colors (Figure 7-9, parts B and C).

**Figure 7-9** ◀

Setting solid color
background options

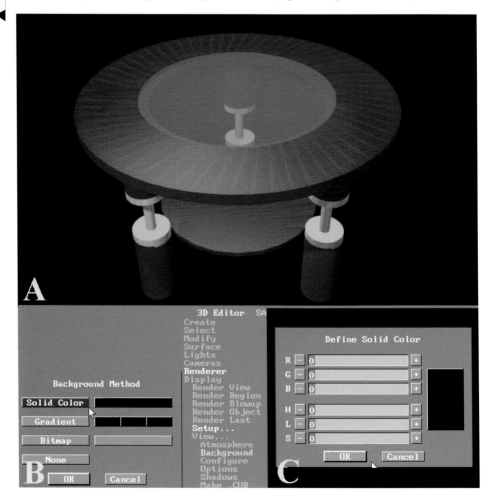

The background assigned to Figure 7-10, part A, is a gradient. In a gradient background, three chosen colors are blended where they meet one another. The gradient can be variations of one hue or three distinct hues, as in this image. The gradient background works well for an image where the focus is not solely on the modeled or rendered object but on the overall presentation of a work. Click on **Render\Setup\Background**. Then highlight the **Gradient** bar on the Background Method panel. Click on the three black bars, and you will get the Define Gradient Colors panel, which allows you to change the background colors (Figure 7-10, parts B and C).

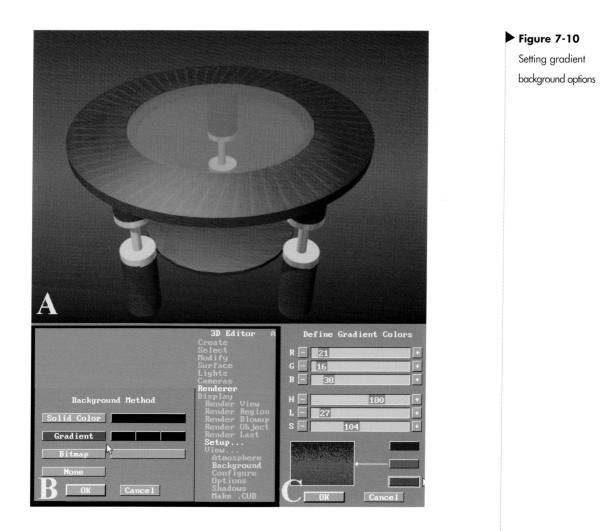

▶ **Figure 7-10**

Setting gradient background options

Figure 7-11, part A, uses a bitmap background. The bitmap puts the image of a saved file behind the object of focus. Bitmap backgrounds serve many purposes, including filling in the view out the windows of a rendered building. In rendering a restaurant, for example, it would be very time-consuming to model all the buildings surrounding the restaurant to complete the window views. It is much easier to assign a bitmap view as background. Click on **Render\Setup\Background**. Then highlight the Bitmap bar on the Background Method panel. Click on the long dark gray bar. You will get the Bitmap for the Rendered Background panel, which allows you to choose the background images (Figure 7-11, parts B and C).

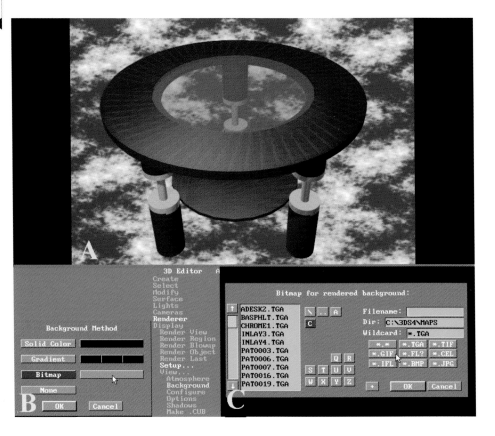

**Figure 7-11**

Setting bitmap background options

## Simulations of the Aging Eye

Because of changes in the eyes, older individuals require more light to see. The rendition of colors is affected by the yellowing, and clouding of the iris in the eye reduces depth perception. The computer can be adjusted by lowering the light levels and by adding an atmosphere of yellow-tinted fog into the space, which will wash out some of the colors and will haze over the depth and three-dimensionality in the environment (Figures 7-12 and 7-13).

▶ **Figure 7-12**

Aging eye

simulation I

**Figure 7-13** ◀

Aging eye
simulation II

**Figure 7-14** ◀

Setting fog options
for aging eye
simulation

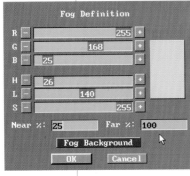

To adjust the light sources choose the following: **Lights\Omni** or **Spot\Adjust**. Click on each individual source and lower the multiplier. For example, if the multiplier is set to the default of 1.0, change it to 0.7. This will reduce the power of the light source in the scene. Ambient lights can be turned down with the Luminance (L) slider. To adjust the atmosphere, choose **Renderer\Setup\Atmosphere\Fog**. Add **Fog** to the scene. Define it to a yellow color (settings of R-255, G-168, and B-31), and set the percentages of fog near 15 percent and far 85 percent (Figure 7-14).

The fog acts as a filter for the light and the colors of the materials in the space. Since environments vary, it is recommended that test renderings be generated and any necessary adjustments be made to the settings.

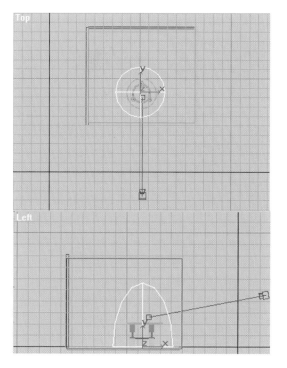

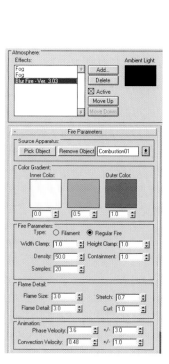

## Simulations of Smoke and Fire

This study involves the use of 3D Studio Max for the simulation creation. If you use 3D Studio R4, you may instead follow the general process rather than the step-by-step process.

Open 3D Studio Max and load the **TAB_FIR1.MAX** file from the CD-ROM. To begin this exercise, go to the **Create\Helpers\Atmospheric Apparatus** and click the button labeled Combustion. Click on the center of the table in the Top viewport, and drag to create the combustion apparatus, making sure to click the Hemisphere box on the side menu. Use the scale tools to scale the apparatus so that it resembles Figure 7-15. After the apparatus is properly scaled, go to the **Render\Environment** pull-down menu and choose Add in the Environment menu. From the Add menu choose **Blur Fire** or **Combustion**, if you do not have the Blur Fire plugged in. From the Environment\Blur Fire menu, click the Pick-Object button and click on the apparatus in any viewport to select it. Copy the settings from Figure 7-16 to the Environment\Blur Fire menu.

Once the fire is in place, you can begin to create the lighting. Begin by going to the **Create\Lights** menu and selecting **Omni**. Click in the Top viewport to place the light in the scene. Use the Top and the Left viewport to position the light according to Figure 7-17. Adjust the light settings to match the ones in Figure 7-18. Repeat this process for the next two lights. For Omni02 make sure to click the Exclude button in the **Modify** menu and exclude the floor from illumination. For Omni03 exclude everything except the floor.

Now that the lights are adjusted, it's time to add smoke to the scene. To do this, go to the Render\Environment menu and choose **Add**. From the Add menu choose **Fog**, and adjust the settings to match Figure 7-19. Repeat the process to add a second fog. Finally, click the Render button, and choose Single at 320 x 240; make sure to choose Save File if you want the rendering to be saved. The final rendering should look similar to Figure 7-20.

**Figure 7-17** ◀

Positioning first light

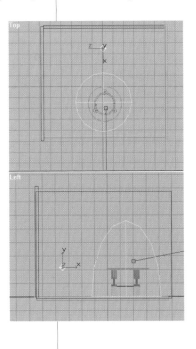

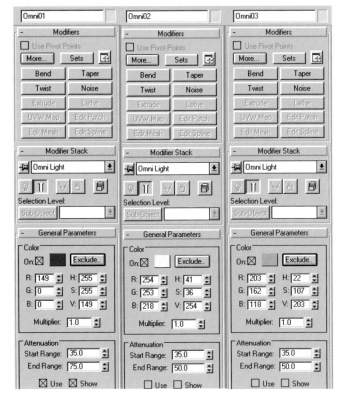

**Figure 7-18** ◀

Setting for all

three lights

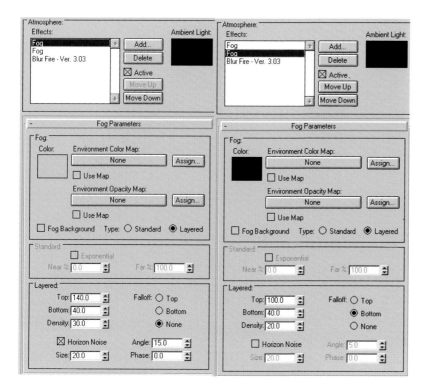

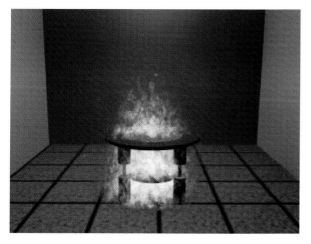

▶ **Figure 7-19**
Settings for first and second fog layers

▶ **Figure 7-20**
Final rendering for smoke and fire simulation

## A 3D and 2D Composition Exercise

### Making Adjustments in 3D Studio Max

This tutorial covers the steps involved in combining a 3D model with a 2D image of an interior. This type of composition allows objects to be presented in an environment where they do not actually exist. Furthermore, although some situations require the background environment to be modeled entirely in 3D, it is often sufficient (and in many cases cost-effective) to model only the new object and use a still 2D image of an existing environment. For example, if both the end table from this tutorial and the background image did not exist in reality, then both would have to be modeled on the computer. This, however, is an extremely complex and time-consuming process. If, however, as is the case in this tutorial, only the end table is imaginary and the environment (in this case an interior) exists in reality, it is much easier and more productive to use the following technique to compose the 3D modeled table and the 2D image of the interior together. For an overview of the composition process, see Figure 7-21.

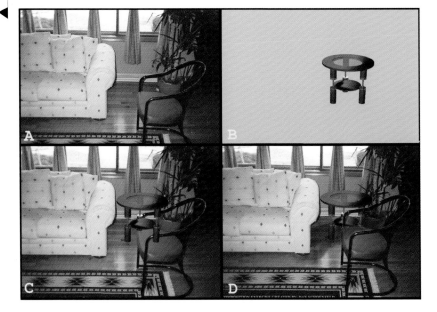

**Figure 7-21** ◀

Overview of the composition process

The first step in combining the table and the background image uses 3D Studio Max to orient and light the table relative to the background image. If you use 3D Studio, you may need to follow only the creation procedure, but not the specific steps.

Start 3D Studio Max and open the **TABLE.MAX** file in CD-ROM CH7 directory TAB_COM folder on the CD. Pull down the Rendering menu and select **Environment**. Then open the **Material Editor**. In the Environment menu, click the **Assign** button and choose **Bitmap** from the list. Click the **Map# bitmap** button, and choose **OK** to accept the default settings. Click the black square under Background Color, and use the slider to change the color to white; then close the Environment menu.

In the Material Editor make sure that slot #1 is active and chose **Screen** as the mapping type.

Under the bitmap parameters section click on the blank **Bitmap** button. Find the 3DMAX\ Maps directory and choose **TAB_COM.TIF** on the CD. Close the Material Editor panel.

One of the main differences between Max and AutoCAD is the ability to move, rotate, and scale objects with absolute precision. It is therefore necessary to employ a bit of creativity, ingenuity, and common sense to complete the next section. Keep in mind that although diagrams of the table and lights have been provided, they are only relative locations and should be used as such. To fine-tune the position, scale, and orientation of the table and lights, it will be necessary to render every time a change is made.

From the Top viewport, move the table along the Y axis until it appears to be in the correct location relative to the couch and the chair. In the Front viewport stretch the table along the Y axis until it appears to be the right size relative to the other objects in the background. It might be necessary to use a combination of stretch and uniform scales in order to maintain the relative proportions of the table. In the Top viewport, rotate the table along the X axis until the table appears to be parallel to the floor in the background. Go to the Command panel and click the **Create** button and then the **Lights** button. Choose **Directional** and click in the Top viewport to create the first light, which will represent the sunlight coming from the window in the background image. While the directional light is selected, click the **Modify** button. Change the settings in the Modify menu to match those in Figure 7-22. Also move and rotate the light, using Figure 7-23 as a guide.

Selecting **Omni** instead of Directional, repeat the previous steps for the remaining three lights, making sure to use Figures 7-22 and 7-23 for the correct settings. When the table is positioned, render the scene to a file as follows: In the Render Scene\Render Output dialogue box, click the **Files...** button. Select a directory where you want to save the rendering. Select **.tif** from the List Files of Type menu.

**Figure 7-22** ◀

Setting all
four lights

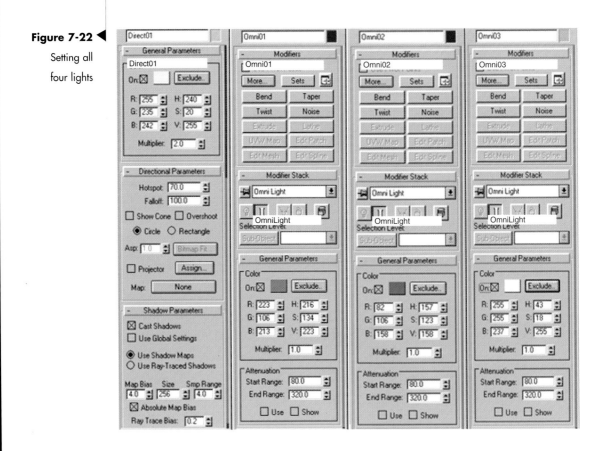

Name the file **Table2.tif** and click **OK** to return to Render Scene. Click the **Render** button to begin rendering the scene. Choose **Environment** from the Rendering menu, and click in the **Use Map** box to turn off the background image. Close the Environment menu. Repeat the rendering steps, making sure to specify a new file name, **Table3.tif**, in the Render Scene menu, and render the scene again.

▶ **Figure 7-23**

Positioning information for all four lights

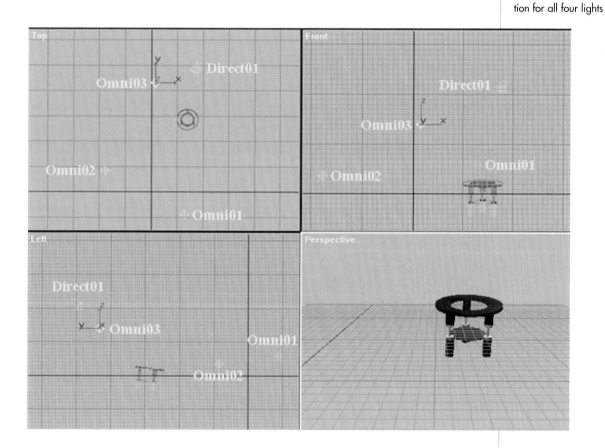

That concludes the 3D Studio Max portion of this tutorial; the remaining steps will be completed in Photoshop. Although the following section is significantly more precise than the previous section, there are a few steps which will require a creative touch in using the diagrams as a general guide.

### Move into Photoshop

Start Photoshop and open **TABLE1.TIF** from the CD-ROM CH7 directory TAB_COMP folder and **TABLE2.TIF** and **TABLE3.TIF**, which should look like the images you created in the previous section. From the Tools palette click the Lasso button and click to unchecked **Anti-aliasing** in the Options palette. Compare the Table1.tif and Table2.tif files to determine how much of the chair is overlapping the table.

In the **TABLE1.TIF** file, hold down the [Alt] key and click to select the portion of the chair which overlaps the table. Make sure to select only the chair, and not the floor or background. It is only necessary to select the portion of the chair which overlaps the table, not the whole chair. When the chair is selected, choose **Copy** from the Edit menu; then from the Edit menu choose Paste to Layer. In the **Paste to Layer** dialogue box, change the name to **Chair**. Click on the Chair layer to make it active; if the portion of the chair that is on the Chair layer does not line up with the chair on the Background layer, do the following (if it does line up, skip to the next step):

If necessary, reselect the chair using the rectangular selection tool. (In this instance it is not necessary to be precise; just make sure to include the entire chair in the selection.)

Move the chair until it lines up with the portion of the chair on the Background layer (if done correctly, the chair should appear to be whole again). Click the title bar of **Table3.tif** to make it active. From the Select menu choose **Select all**. From the Edit menu choose **Copy**. Click the title bar of **Table1.tif** to make the file active. From the Edit menu choose Paste to layer. In the **Paste to Layer** dialogue box, change the name to **Table**. Click the Table layer to make it active. From the Tools palette, click the **Magic wand** button. In the Options palette, set the Tolerance to **1** and make sure the Anti-aliasing box is checked. Use the

Magic Wand tool to click anywhere on the white background to select it. From the Select menu, choose **Select similar** and hit the [Delete] key.

Note that last several steps are designed to maintain the position of the table relative to the background image. Had those steps been done before the table was pasted to the Table1.tif file, the table would not have appeared in its correct position, defeating much of the careful positioning and lighting done in 3D Studio MAX. It is therefore important that these steps be completed in proper order.

For the table to appear to be behind the chair, it may be necessary to change the order of the layers in the Layers palette. If this is indeed necessary, simply click and drag the layers up or down to change their order. The order of the layers from top to bottom should be Chair, Table, and Background. Click the title bar of **Table2.tif** to make it active. In the Tools palette, click the **Rectangular selection** button. In the Options palette, select **Elliptical** from the pull-down menu. Using the Elliptical selection tool, select the glass portion of the tabletop, making sure to include some of the wood (here again, it is not necessary to be precise). From the Edit menu choose **Copy**.

Click the title bar of **Table1.tif** to make it active. From the Edit menu, choose **Paste to Layer** and do not give this layer a name. In the Layers palette, click the layer without a name to make it active. Reselect the tabletop if necessary, and carefully position the selected top so that it covers the top on the Table layer. It is important to position the top correctly so that the table appears to be whole, with the glass having the correct transparency showing. In the Layers palette, click the **Eye** icon next to all the layers except the Table layer and the layer with no name. (The Eye icons turn layers on and off.) In the Layers palette, click on the **Right arrow** button and select **Merge**. In the Paste to Layer dialogue box, change the name to **Table**. Click the **Eye** icons to turn on all the layers.

The last steps are designed to minimize the number of layers in the file. Although layers are remarkably useful, unfortunately each additional layer increases the size of the file significantly. Wherever possible, it is always preferable to maintain as small a file as possible.

The following shadowing procedure is the most imprecise part of this section. Placing shadows correctly in a scene requires a reasonably advanced understanding of light and shadow. Unfortunately, imparting such a level of understanding is somewhat beyond the scope of this tutorial. Instead, use Figure 7-24 as a guide for comparison to gain a better understanding of what areas have received shadows.

**Figure 7-24**

Final rendering for table composition

In the Tools palette, click the **Dropper** button. Click on the Table layer to make it active, and click on the shadowed area of the table. The foreground color will change to reflect the color that you have selected with the dropper. In the Layers palette, click on the **New layer** button to create a new layer. Name the new layer **Shadow**, and if necessary, move it to the top of the Layers stack. In the Layers palette, click to make the Shadow layer active. In the Tools palette, click the **Lasso** button and select the first area to be shadowed. In the Tools palette, click the **Paintbucket** button and click to fill the selected area. In the Layers palette, use the Opacity slider and change the opacity to 53 percent. In the Tools palette, click the Smudge button. In the Options palette, change the pressure to 22 percent. Press the [Control] and [D] keys to deselect the filled area. Use the **Smudge** tool to smudge and spread the edges of the filled area. Repeat the last five steps until shadowing is complete.

Click on the **New layer** button in the Layers palette. Name the new layer **Text** and if necessary, move it to the top of the Layers stack. In the Layers palette, click the Text layer to make it active. In the Tools palette, click the Text button and click anywhere in the file to begin creating text. Choose a size and style, type any text you wish in the box, and click **OK**. Position the text in an appropriate location. (If the text does stand out well enough against the background, delete the text, change the foreground color, and then repeat the text process.)

## Summary

This tutorial has demonstrated how to integrate, using the basic tool sets of 3D Studio, 3D Studio MAX, and Photoshop. It is possible to effectively simulate numerous environmental conditions as well as learn to combine the advantages of each software package to achieve a desired goal. It is through the evolution of these and other techniques that the application of rendering has shifted from only representing the final design solution under ideal conditions to becoming a simulation, evaluation, and creation tool. Different approaches to rendering need to be adapted to their intended purposes within the design process. In the near future, designers with increasing digital knowledge, more powerful computers, and more intelligent software will be able to visualize a proposed design in truly scientific fashion.

University of Wisconsin – Madison Chemistry Building, Study Image

**Flad & Associates**

# THE FOURTH DIMENSION: USING 3D ANIMATION IN INTERIOR DESIGN VISUALIZATION

**8**

*In the dream state we can create any reality we wish. Sometimes we even take these dreams and mold them into the reality of a building, a painting, a sculpture, or an interior, so as to allow others to experience our vision. With the incredible advancements in 3D computer animation techniques, it is now possible to share our design experience with others even before they become a physical reality.*

> *The best approach to computer visualization is not to mimic the style of traditional renderings or emulate the realism of photographs, but to communicate design concepts in ways that physical models or renderings cannot. This usually does not involve realism, but instead abstraction, disassembly, and motion.*
>
> *- K. Sanders*

# Introduction

The unique opportunity to experience and evaluate an environment through time before it is built gives designers, architects, and prospective clients an invaluable insight into a proposed project. In fact, by combining 3D digital modeling and rendering techniques with computer animation, 3D animation is quickly becoming the most effective visualization format in all design-related fields.

If we believe movement and experience are important elements in architectural and interior design, then how can the medium approximate the human experience in space and time before it has been built? This is a critical challenge to the development of design representation. The search for methods to represent movement in design has never stopped. For example, before introducing video camera technology into an architectural design, designers draw a continuous panoramic image (Figure 8-1) or take a series of photos and then assemble them to represent the totality of a space through motion. "Motion provides an additional perspective clue. This visual information can be depicted by a sequence of pictures, or pictures seen from slightly different points. . . . They provide depth cues not available in still pictures" (Sanoff, 1991, p.13).

In recent history, designers and architects have used model simulators, video cameras, and computer-generated composite images to assist in effectively communicating and presenting the design concept through motion. In physical model simulation, some of the traditional tools are video cameras, film, and slides. Movement is created through a sequential documentation of a scale model with video cameras. With a periscope device attached to a video camera, it is possible to locate the viewpoint at eye level in the space model and then to provide movement by moving the camera within the space. The video could then be utilized as an effective method of presentation and design communication.

Specifically, in a study at the University of Lundt in Sweden, a "video camera . . . was attached to a periscope device. This scope or snorkel located the viewpoint very close to the model surface, allowing images to be taken from a height identical to the driver's or pedestrian's eye height" (Burden, 1985, p. 76). Quite often, the video camera is driven by stepping motors, providing movements in all three directions and controlled over a video monitor. The operator controls the movements of the video camera with a steering wheel, very similar to driving a car (p. 76). There are other types of model simulators which are ". . . relatively complex and require a trained operator. The system,

A.

B.

C.

▶ **Figure 8-1**

Continuous panoramic image: Iowa State University campus

A.                          B.                          C.

*"Well-choreographed animation, in fact, is one of the most compelling forms of digital media available to the architect"*

*(Sanders, 1996, p. 174)*

therefore, is used mainly for research and commercial projects. The camera is driven through the model by setting a certain speed for the stepping motor device" (p. 80). The University of California at Berkeley, Massachusetts Institute of Technology, and architectural schools in Holland have done extensive research in the use of video simulation in design.

So far, many traditional approaches to simulation, including model simulation, are beneficial as final presentation tools but often not easy for design evaluation and manipulation. The shape, size, and material of the physical models were presented in the finished stage of the design. Also, the lighting was used only to create an effect to enhance the video and did not have any relationship to the actual proposed design.

In other design fields, such as engineering, the idea of using computers to simulate objects and environments for evaluation purposes has been around since the late 1950s. In 1958 IBM joined forces with General Motors to develop a system that would allow designers at GM to use computer-generated 3D models to evaluate prototype vehicles. The result of the IBM-GM partnership was the Design Augmented by Computers (DAC-1). The system allowed the

designers at GM to input a 3D description of a vehicle and then rotate it in any direction. The system was finally unveiled in 1964 at the Joint Computer Conference in Detroit. In the 1960s, scientific 3D visualization was being done at Massachusetts Institute of Technology. It was not until the mid 1980s that scientific, particularly molecular, visualization would begin to take shape. By the late 1980s and early 1990s virtually every major industry was in some way involved with 3D animation.

The fairly recent introduction of 3D animation into the fields of architecture and interior design has created many new and exciting possibilities for today's architects and designers. The boundaries of designing architectural interiors are no longer limited to three dimensions but extend to the fourth dimension. This fourth dimension involves motion and changing views, with a sense of space and personal involvement in space. Animation, as a format for evaluation, visualization, and representation, provides a closer link between design development and reality. With the increasing quality of hardware and software for CAD and the new concept of using computers in design, it is likely that animated visualization will become a very effective tool in the future of architectural and interior design.

Office lobby, two views

**Strang Inc.**

# Concepts

## Motion in Architectural and Interior Design

"Architecture, as with all art, is fundamentally confronted with questions of human existence in space and time, expressing and relating man's being in the world" (Pallasmaa, 1996, p. 8). A person's experience of an environment and his or her movement through that environment is a multisensory experience which strengthens his or her sense of what is the real world. And architecture, which gives matter, space, and scale to our environment, is an extension of "nature into the man-made realm." Furthermore, "an architectural work is not experienced as a collection of isolated visual pictures. . . . Instead of mere vision, or the five classical senses, architecture involves several realms of sensory experience which interact and fuse into each other" (Pallasmaa, 1996, p. 28, 30).

*"All architecture functions as a potential stimulus for movement. A building is an incitement to action, a stage for movement, and interaction. It is one partner in a dialogue with the body" (Bloomer & More, 1977, p.59).*

Architectural and interior design is the experience of movement in a sequence of spaces. As today's environment becomes more and more complex, designers have to deal with a variety of problems that may or may not have been studied in the past. To ensure a successful design, there are critical processes which help the designer to better understand motion in design and to facilitate the travel through the proposed architectural and interior design before it is built. "Even Le Corbusier admitted to the many surprises which he had encountered after the completion of his buildings – visual anomalies which had not been anticipated nor accounted for within his design sequence" (Porter, 1979, p. 91). Therefore, it is essential to attempt a visual simulation of movement within a space. "It is this ability to simulate motion, which is vital, for at the essence of our understanding of space is our movement within it" (p. 91).

## Creating Motion With the Computer

In order to create motion, there are two options. First, you can go to each frame individually and modify the scene. For example, if you have a 30-frame animation and you wish to move a sphere from one side of the screen to another, you can go to every frame and move the sphere a little farther across the screen. When the animation is played, the sphere will appear to travel across the screen. This is a fine method if your animation is only 30 frames long; this, however, is rarely the case. If you have a long animation, you may employ the second method of animation, known as keyframing. **Keyframes** are the frames in an animation that mark the beginning and ending states of an action. Turning again to the 30-second sphere animation, instead of going to every frame, you can go to several key positions and move the sphere to its final position. The computer will then calculate the position of the sphere in all the frames in between. Back when manual animation was the only option, the best animators would create the most important frames, or keyframes, and their underlings would generate the in-between frames, the **tweens**, which are the frames in between keyframes (Figure 8-2). Using 3D Studio MAX, or a similar software package for animation, we set up the keyframes and the computer generates the tweens. As a general rule, the more complex an animation is, the more keyframes are needed.

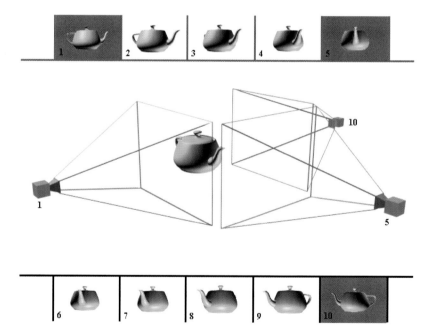

▶ **Figure 8-2**

The keyframing process

185

## The Dimensions of a Pathway

When traveling in a space or looking at a 3D object, we need a direction, a way to formalize a pathway so we can experience and circulate through the space as well as reach our destination. The nature of the path had not been fully explored in design visualization until digital media arrived. In comparison with all other media for design representation, the concept of a path is one of the most unique elements in 3D animation.

"The path of our movement can be conceived as the perceptual thread that links the spaces of a building, or any series of interior or exterior spaces, together. Since we move in Time through a Sequence of Spaces, we experience a space in relation to where we've been and where we anticipate going" (Ching, 1996, p. 228). When we are designing, we are searching for the best pathway for mentally traveling through the design. But the nature of the path has always been difficult to represent in a design document as well as hard to communicate to others.

Studying the major elements of the pathway for a building may help us understand how we can best walk through a proposed design. In other words, what are the major views we need to include in the animation to have the most communication value. In *Architecture: Form, Space, and Order*, Professor Ching (1996) has included five elements important for experiencing a sequence of spaces: approach, entrance, configuration of the path, path-space relationship, and form of circulation (see Figure 8-3).

The **approach** is ". . . the first phase of the circulation system, during which we are prepared to see, experience, and use the spaces within a building. The approach to a building and its entrance may vary in duration from a few paces through a compressed space to a lengthy and circuitous route. It may be perpendicular to the primary facade of a building or be oblique to it" (Ching, 1996, p. 230 ). When we set up a camera to start the architectural walk-through, we should consider the design which will have the most compelling effect. Should we choose a straight path to a space that enhances a design which features geometric shapes, or should we use a curvilinear path to reflect the relaxing and organic shapes of the building which encourages wandering leisurely before entering the space?

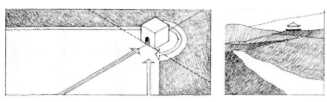

Approach: The Distant View

Entrance: From Outside to Inside

Configuration of the Path: The Sequence of Spaces

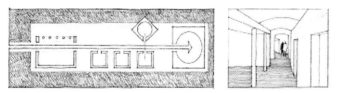

Path-space Relationships: Edges, Nodes, and Terminations of the Path

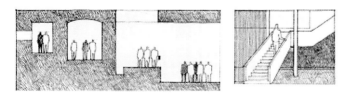

Form of the Circulation Space: Corridors, Galleries, Stairways and Rooms

▶ **Figure 8-3**

Key elements of the pathway

Images from *Architecture: Form, Space, and Order* by Francis D.K. Ching, 1996. Reprinted by permission of John Wiley & Sons, Inc.

The **entrance** ". . . involves the act of penetrating a vertical plane that distinguishes one space from another and separates 'here' from 'there'" (Ching, 1996, p. 238). When translating this concept to a computer walk-through, creating several frames of animation is most valuable to clarify the transition between the passage from the exterior environment, over the threshold, and into the interior space. First, the camera view may provide a limited panoramic view, and then a more narrowly defined view to represent the entrance area into the new space.

The **configuration of a path** ". . . both influences and is influenced by the organizational pattern of the spaces it links. . . . Once we are able to map out in our minds the overall configuration of the paths in a building, our orientation within the building and our understanding of its spatial layout will be made clear" (Ching, 1996, p. 252). Keeping this thought in mind while setting the path of the architectural walk-through, the designer should have a clear picture of the organization of spaces. For instance, the designer should be noting where the major and secondary hallways are, what is the best view for the intersections of the hallways, and what is the sequence for experiencing the large and small spaces. The path should facilitate the use of the area with consideration for the variety of people who use the space. Figure 8-4 shows the different pathways describing a sequence of spaces.

The **path-space relationships** can be defined in several ways: pass by spaces, pass through spaces, and terminate in a space. Since paths link spaces in a variety of ways, the designer should decide what the priorities are. When we walk through with the camera we note that some paths function as only a link between spaces while maintaining the integrity of the spaces. The path simply passes by a space without entering or intruding on the space. Another configuration might be a path that passes through a space, creating patterns of movement within the space. Finally, a path may terminate in a space which ultimately has established the main function of the path and where the camera pans the surrounding environment (Ching, 1996, p. 264).

The **form of circulation** which a space accommodates, can be studied as the experience of different shapes, volume, height, size, and texture. The camera viewpoints, essential to the correct representation of the features of the space, should include the wide variety of different forms found there. The animation also should reflect the experience of people in motion as they walk along, pause, rest, or take in a view along a path.

There are a number of ways movement can be brought into a scene. Different kinds of objects can be animated in different ways. For example, individual objects can move or change their size and shape; lights can change position, brightness, and color; or a camera can move around a path, giving different views of a scene. These techniques are discussed in the Applications section of this chapter.

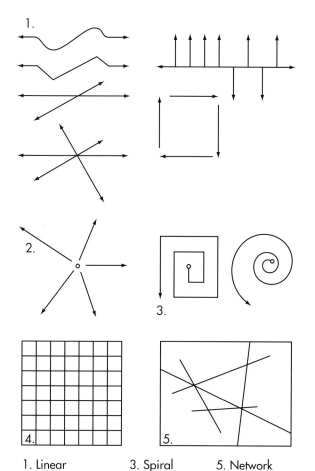

**▶ Figure 8-4**

Different pathways

Images from *Architecture: Form, Space, and Order* by Francis D.K. Ching, 1996. Reprinted by permission of John Wiley & Sons, Inc.

1. Linear      3. Spiral      5. Network
2. Radial      4. Grid        6. Composite

# Cognition

## Organizing the Animation

The first step in organizing a 3D animation is the creation of a storyboard, as explained for 2D animation. Similar to the storyboards used in movies and commercials, the animation storyboard is a 2D representation of the most important frames within the animation sequence. Additionally, the animation storyboard contains technical information about transition, special effects, cameras, and movement. The next step in the organizational process involves experimentation with different elements of the animation. Often this means creating short test animations of the key sequences of the animation. When the experimentation phase has been satisfactorily completed, it is time to create the whole animation.

## Speed in Motion

In the book *Color Model Environments*, Harold Linton (1985) proposed rate of speed as one of the dimensions of movement. The rate "may be considered fast, slow, or any intermediate speed and has a pronounced expressive value. The rate can be a constant, or it can be altered in a regular progression abruptly. Changes similar to these can also become part of the pattern of larger rhythms" (p.174).

In computer animation, the speed of the motion can be set by the designer. The change of rate can be achieved by making the adjustment of the frames. In viewing from here to there, more frames result in a smoother motion. The computer animation, represented by a series of still images or frames, produces the illusion of movement when viewed in quick succession. The illusion of motion by a computer-generated animation is the same one used in film: when a sequence of still frames is displayed quickly enough to the eye, the mind perceives motion. The fluidity of the motion depends on how fast the individual frames are displayed and the amount of motion. The speed of the animation is measured in frames per second (fps). In film, the camera samples the scene 24 times a second. In video, the camera samples the scene 30 times a second. Most desktop computers display digital animation at a slower rate, from 10 to 20 fps, although their performance is increasing each year.

## Seeing through a Camera

The video camera has helped the designer to record motion in physical model simulation. "The eye and the camera may have basic functions in common with one another; however, there are enormous differences between them. For example, the eye has the ability to perceive movement in clearly defined images without the need of a shutter" (Linton, 1985, p.199).

The camera's complex setting in the digital environment, including changing the lens or the focus, generates perspectives or adjusts the ranges, but the camera is still not the same as our eyes. When our eyes move from one place to another, they change focus as they pan from object to object, but we do not need to stop the viewing process. The spaces are immobile. To an observer, the appearance of a space or the experiences of spaces do change because the observer is capable of motion. We traditionally build a scale model to represent our design and use a camera to record the views of the observer. Now we use the computer to build the model and assign a camera to simulate a person's vision. The camera in an architectural walk-through directly influences the effect of the simulation.

The concept of the camera in digital media has more sophisticated features than earlier techniques using video cameras and brings us one step closer to simulating the function of human eyes in real situations. The **field of view** (FOV) of the human eye is almost twice as large as the FOV of a camera. In addition, the peripheral areas of human vision are blurred in such a way as to subconsciously filter visual information, something which cannot be reproduced using a camera.

Human vision is stereoscopic (involving two eyes), resulting in both a wider FOV and a distinct impression of three-dimensionality within the environment. When a real environment is perceived by human eyes, the images sent to the brain are not processed as still images and then discarded, but rather the images are saved and joined together to form a true 360° impression of the surrounding environment. On the other hand, when an environment is viewed through a camera, the images tend to be discarded much more quickly, resulting in a more disjointed impression of the environment.

When viewed, through human eyes, objects tend to move in and out of focus, both consciously and unconsciously. This minimizes the amount of information that has to be processed while still giving an overall impression of an environment. A camera image, however, must be processed in its entirety for an impression of the environment to be formed.

## Walk-through of a Prebuilt Environment under Normal Conditions

Architectural **walk-throughs** are a common and increasingly popular way for designers to visualize and express their work and ultimately sell their design to a client. To create a walk-through of a design space, an environment is modeled and rendered under what we have termed "ideal" or "normal" conditions. The animation gives the illusion of moving through the space, expressing what it would be like to literally walk through the design space before it is built. Obviously, the experience is not the same as the experience of a built space, but a computer-generated walk-through can provide a lot of visual and spatial information for the designer and client.

The illusion is created by setting up a camera and literally moving it through the space as if the camera were a person moving and looking around at the different spatial features. Architectural walk-throughs can be one of the easiest types of animations to construct because there is usually only one type of motion to add, that which changes the position of the camera. Depending upon the goal of the animation, the camera can be set up differently.

The effect of the visual walk-through can be a dramatic and effective selling tool for a space, but it is not how a space will be realistically viewed by users after an environment is built. It is impossible to understand and build a truly realistic animation of the experience of a space, since every individual experiences and interacts with space differently. However, there are some tricks to creating a walk-through, which will help with a realistic impression. These are discussed in the Applications section. Both free cameras and target cameras are useful for the task. **Free camera** is for views of the area in the direction that the camera is aimed. This type of camera is most often used for animating along a path. The **target camera** is used for viewing the area around a target object. This type of camera can be used when you want the camera to always follow an object, regardless of where it is in the scene.

## Walk-through of a Prebuilt Environment under Special Conditions

Just as special conditions are created with still-image renderings, they can also be created in an architectural walk-through. Using animation techniques, we can simulate a power failure and visually analyze whether the user of the space would be able to see exit doors. We can analyze how aging eyes would see the space and can look for hazards such as steps or level changes that are not easily discernible.

# Applications

## Light Fixture Animation

The animation of objects can range in complexity from the addition of one simple movement to several complex movements, starting and ending at different times during the animation. For this exercise we will build a swing arm lamp (Figure 8-5).

Once the lamp has been modeled we are ready to add its movement. Before beginning the animation, examine the lamp and identify the following items: (1) the source of the movement, (2) which parts need to move individually, and (3) which parts need to be linked to move together.

**Figure 8-5** ◄

Finished lamp

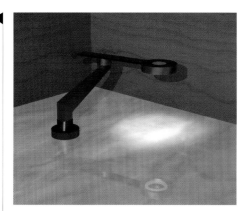

Upon examining the swing arm lamp, two sources of movement are identified: the cylinder attaching the lower arm to the lamp base and the cylinder connecting the upper arm to the lower arm. When the cylinder connecting the base to the lower arm is rotated, everything above this cylinder needs to rotate with it. This includes the lower arm form, the upper arm form, the lamp fixture, and the light source. When the cylinder connecting the upper arm to the lower arm is rotated, the upper arm, the light fixture, and the light source must move, but the lower arm and base must be unaffected.

Start by opening 3D Studio MAX and load **LAMP.MAX** file from the attached CD in the CH8\Lamp directory.

To link the object, use the Select and Link button (Figure 8-6). To see the names of the objects used in this scene refer to Figure 8-7. To begin, click on the **_lamptop_** group to select it and click the **Select and Link** button to activate it (when active, the button will turn green). Hold the cursor over **_lamptop_**; it should appear as two white cubes chained together. Click and hold the left mouse button while dragging the cursor downward to **_cyl-arm_**. The upper cube on the cursor should turn green. When it does, release the mouse button (if the link is successful, **_cyl-arm_** will flash white to indicate that it is now linked). To perform the next link, select **_cyl-arm_** and repeat the previous process, extending the white cubes over the **_arm-bas_** until one turns green. For the last link select **_arm-bas_** and repeat the linking process.

▶ **Figure 8-6**
3D Studio MAX
toolbar

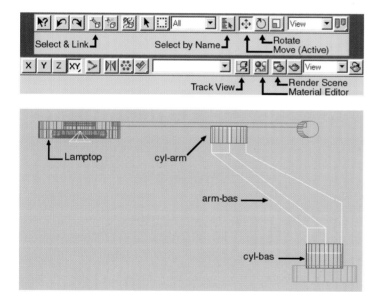

▶ **Figure 8-7**
Lamp components

After all of the linkages are in place, we are ready to animate the lamp. The animation will be a minimum of 60 frames to allow one full rotation of the lamp. We will keyframe 90° of rotation every 15 frames for one full 360° rotation. To begin, select the **_cyl-bas_** and choose the Top viewport by clicking on its name. Click on the large **Animate** button in the lower right hand corner of the screen (it should turn red when active). In the white box to the right of the **Animate** button highlight the **_0_** and type **_15_** and be sure to hit **Enter** to move the slider to **15**. Click the **Rotate** button to make it active and from the **EDIT** menu, choose **Transform Type-In** (the **Rotate Transform Type-In** panel should appear). In the Offset: Screen portion of the panel in the box next to the **Z**, highlight the **0.0** and type 90; then hit **Enter**. Continue changing the **Z** value in the Transform Type-In panel by 90° for every 15 frames up to 60. Now select the *cyl-arm* and repeat the same animation process using *−90°* in the **Z** section of the Transform Type-In panel. Now turn off the **Animate** button and play the animation in the viewport. Notice that the lamp stops rotating after frame 60. To make the lamp continue rotating, we can do one of two things. First, we can continue keyframing every 15 frames until the end of the animation. Second, we can use one of the Parameter Curve Out-of-Range Type *Controllers* which, when applied, can make the single 360° rotation that we keyframed already repeat automatically for the entire length of the animation.

To render your animation, click on the **Render Scene** button to open the Render Scene panel. In the Time output section of the panel, click the **Range** button and and enter the range of frames that have been animated (i.e., 0 to 60). In the Output Size section of the panel, set the size at **320 x 240**, which will decrease render time as well as file size (to play smoothly at higher resolution, the computer must maintain a minimum transfer rate of 30 Mbit/sec). Leave the default settings in the Options section. In Render Output make sure to *uncheck* the Virtual Frame Buffer box and then click the **Files** button. Choose a file name and location and choose **OK**. When prompted, choose a **Compressor**. The higher the compression, the small the file size and the smoother the animation will play. However, high compression causes a drastic loss in picture quality. When you finish configuring the Render Scene Dialog box, click the **Render** button. To play the animation after it is rendered, open the built-in Media Player, find the file, and choose Open.

## Walk-through under Normal Conditions

In this tutorial we will be using three cameras to create a walk-through for a small restaurant. Each camera is used to highlight a distinct space within the total environment (i.e., bar, dining area, and individual table).

To begin this tutorial, open 3D Max and load the file **WALK_THRU1.MAX** on the CD in the CH8/Walk directory. In the **CREATE** Panel, click on the **Cameras** icon and choose **Target**. Click in the Top viewport to create the first camera and its target. To position the camera, click on the **Select by Name** button from the top tool bar, highlight

both **camera01** and **camera01.target**, and click the **Select** button at the bottom of the menu. Once the camera and target are selected, click on the **Move** button and move the camera up in the Left viewport (Figure 8-8). To create a path for this camera, from the **CREATE** Panel click on the **Shapes** icon and choose **Line**. In the Top viewport, click once to begin the line on the right of the camera. Drag left to stretch the line; then click again to place the end vertex, and right-click once to end the line.

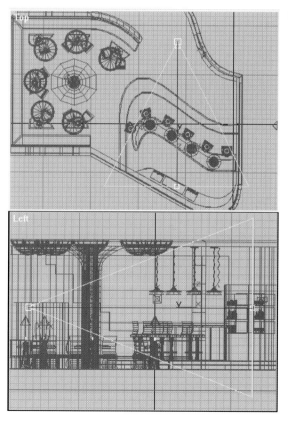

▶ **Figure 8-8**

Position for target
camera01

From the **MODIFY** panel, choose **Edit Spline** (make sure that the Sub-Object button is high-lighted), and in the Top viewport, right-click on either end of the line and choose **Bezier Corner** from the bottom of the list. When the end point turns into a green-ended handle, click and drag the green end to turn the line into a curve (Figure 8-9). To attach the camera to the path, select the camera, and from the **MOTION** panel, click on the **Assign Controller** title bar to open it. From the **Assign Controller** menu, click on the word **Position** to highlight it, and click the green arrow button in the uppermost left-hand corner of the menu. From the Replace Position Controller Panel, choose **Path** from the list and click **OK**. At the bottom of the **MOTION** panel in the Path Parameters section, click **the Pick Path** button, and in the Top viewport, click on the line to select it as the path for the camera.

**Figure 8-9** ◀

Shape and position for Camera01 path

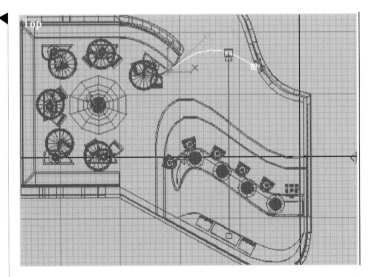

After you assign the path to the camera, the camera should jump down to the floor where the path was created. To reposition the camera, select the path (which the camera is now bound to) and move it upward in the Left viewport. While moving the path in the Left view-port, observe the changes in the *camera01* viewport.

Finally, the movement of the camera along the path needs to be adjusted so that the camera is 100 percent along the path at frame 100. To do this, select the Camera and click on the **Track View** button to open the Track View. In the Track View, click on the **Filters** button, and in the Show Only section check the Selected Objects box and click **OK**.

After the filter has been applied, the line will be shown along with all of the actions (including the path controller) which have been applied to it. Next to the word Percent there will be two dots which represent the beginning and end keyframes for the path. Right-click the second dot, change the 400 to 100 in the Time slot, and close the keyframe and Track View windows (Figure 8-10).

To create the second camera, from the **CREATE** panel click the **Cameras** icon and choose **Free**. Click in the center of the Top viewport to create the free camera. Click on the Left viewport to make it active and select the **Rotate** tool. From the **EDIT** menu, select **Transform Type-In**, and in the Offset Screen Section type **−90** in the **Z** slot. Select the

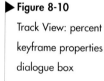

▶ **Figure 8-10**

Track View: percent keyframe properties dialogue box

Left Viewport to make it active and repeat the process using **−90** for the **Z** slot; then close the Transform Type-In box. This will orient the camera correctly to your scene. In the Left viewport move the camera upward to about the middle of the room and rotate the camera to its starting position, using Figure 8-11. Click the **Track View** button to open the Track View and click the **Filters** button. Check the box next to Selected Objects and click **OK**. Click on the plus sign next to **camera02** to expand its Tracks and Transform to expand its tracks. Click on the **Add Keys** button and click once anywhere in the track opposite the word Rotation to set a keyframe.

To adjust the keyframe, click the **Move Keys** button and right-click on the dot. Change the number in the time slot to **100**. Close the keyframe and Track View windows. To animate the rotation of the camera, click on the **Animate** button at the bottom of the screen to active it. Change the frame number to **260** and rotate the camera to its end position (so that it is looking at the opposite side of the room).

Figure 8-11 ◀
Position for free
Camera02

Figure 8-12 ◀
Position for target
Camera03

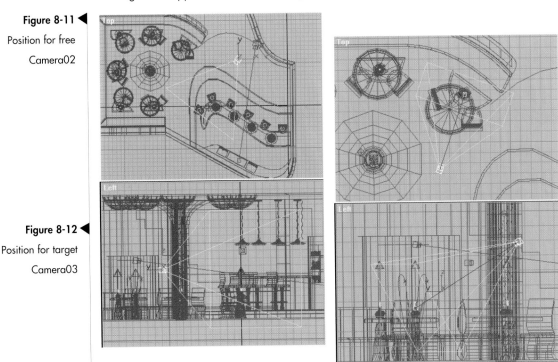

For the third camera, the creation process is the same as the first camera except the path is 3D. Use Figure 8-12 as a reference to create a target camera and move it to about the middle between ceiling and floor. Using the Line tool, create a path with four vertices. Once the path is created (before Edit Spline is applied), move it in the Left viewport until it is at about the same level as the first path. Then in the Top viewport, apply Edit Spline and change the middle two vertex to **bezier** by right-clicking on them. While still in Edit Spline, select the vertice at the end of the path and click on the word **Left** to activate the Left viewport, which will keep the preselected vertex selected. In the Left viewport, move the vertice downward to a position slightly above the tabletop (Figure 8-13). Follow the same procedure as in the first camera to attach the camera to the path. Adjust the percent along the path of the camera by using the Track View and changing the time slot of the first keyframe to **260** .

The final part of this tutorial uses Video Post to render and composite the scene. Video Post is a postproduction software package built into 3D Max. It is very similar to Adobe Premier with the important distinction that, whereas Premier can only edit with prerendered files, Video Post and 3D Max can render and composite a scene in one step.

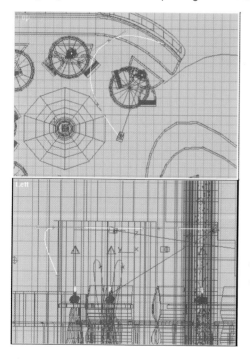

▶ **Figure 8-13**

Shape and position for Camera03 path

From the **RENDERING** menu, choose **Video Post**. In **Video Post**, click on the **Add Scene Event** button and choose *camera01* from the View section drop-down list. In the Video Post Parameters section enter 0 for the VP Start Time and **100** for the VP End Time and click **OK** (Figure 8-14). Repeat the process, select *camera02*, and enter **80** for the VP Start and **220** for the VP End.

In addition, under the Scene Range Section, uncheck the lock to the Video Post Range box and the Lock Range bar to Scene Range box. Enter **100** for the Scene Start and **240** for the Scene End. Select **camera01** and **camera02** by highlighting their names in the Queue list.

Once the cameras are highlighted, click the **Add Image Layer Event** button and choose **Cross Fade Transition** from the Layer Plug-In section. Enter **80** for the cross-faded VP Start and **100** for its VP End (Figure 8-15).

Due to a technical limitation of Video Post, it is necessary to break camera02 into two sections, the first of which you have already added and cross-faded with camera01. Use the Add the Scene Event procedure to add camera02 to the Queue a second time. This time enter **221** for the VP Start and **241** for the VP End. Uncheck the boxes in the Scene Range section and enter **241** for Scene Start and **261** for Scene End; then click **OK**. Follow the Add Scene Event procedure to add camera03 to the Queue using **221** for the VP Start,

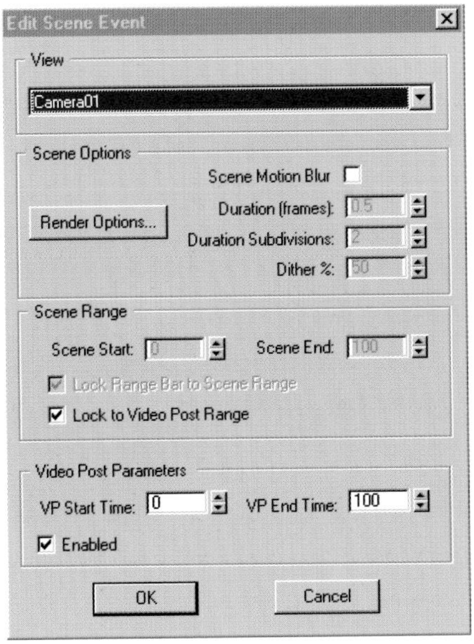

**Figure 8-14** ◀

Video Post: Edit Scene Event dialogue box

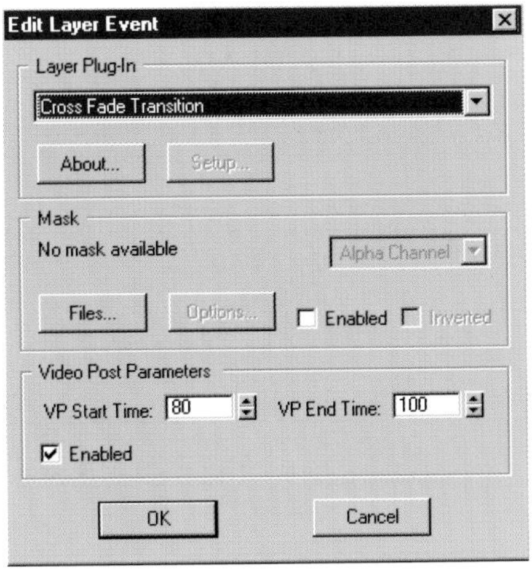

**Figure 8-15** ◀

Video Post: Edit Layer Event dialogue box

360° for the VP End, **261** for Scene Start and **400** for Scene End. Use the same procedure for adding a cross-fade as you did for camera01 and camera02, using **221** for the VP Start and **241** for VP End.

Finally, click the **Add Image Output Event** and click the Files button in the Image **File** section. Choose a name and location for your animation and click **OK**. To render the animation, click on the **Execute Sequence** button and set the image size to 320 x 240 (for testing purposes) in the Output Size section. Then click the **Render** button.

## Walk-through under Special Conditions

Once you know how to create walk-through animations and adjust still images for special conditions (Chapter 7), the skills can be combined to acquire additional information about a proposed environment. Use the file that was used to animate the ideal walk-through conditions, but before modifying anything, save the file under a new name. This way the existing file can be modified for other conditions without losing the original file for the ideal rendering.

First, render an animation file, demonstrating what a walk-through would be like for an individual with aging eyes. The modifications are the ones made earlier to the still-image file, turning down the light level and adding yellow-tinted fog as atmosphere. Refer to the still-image modification for details on making the adjustments. You are now ready to render the animation. Load the **AGING-1.AVI** from the CD CH8 directory as reference.

There are also special adjustments that can be made to test for different things. For example, set up a walk-through to see if the individual would have trouble seeing the level "exit" sign with the power out. Load **POWER-2.AVI** file from the CD CH8 directory for reference.

## Advanced Simulation in a Commercial Environment

### Process

The purpose of the following tutorial is to demonstrate how some of the techniques covered thus far can be combined to create an advanced simulation in a commercial environment. Due to the advanced nature of this project, a step-by-step tutorial is well beyond the scope of this book. Instead, the following will be a procedural tutorial, which will serve as a general outline for this project. As with the other tutorials, two sample files have been provided. The first one, **ADY_SIM1.MAX**, contains only the model of the commercial environment which can be used to begin this tutorial. The second file, **ADV_SIM2.MAX**, is a finished version of the whole simulation, including all the environmental and lighting effects. The last section of this tutorial will show how to use ADV_SIM2.MAX to augment the more general procedures.

In an effort to make things more manageable, the following tutorial is divided into two main sections. The first section will cover the creation of the light study which corresponds to the first 1000 frames of the adv_sim2.max file and the lightsim.avi animation. The second section will deal with creating fire, smoke, and water (sprinklers), which corresponds to the remaining frames of adv_sim2.max and the firesim.avi animation. All the files mentioned previously are stored on the CD. Since this is not a step-by-step tutorial, you may find it helpful to read the whole tutorial before trying any of the procedures.

## Lighting Simulation
### Creating a storyboard

As with any animation, the first step is to create a storyboard. The storyboard should contain information about length, objects, effects, lighting, and camera positions. The information in the storyboard will then give you a solid foundation from which to begin modeling and animating. Furthermore, the storyboard will help you decide which items require attention first. This is important because, although ideally we would like modeling and animation to be a linear process, the reality is that most projects, including this one, are very interactive in nature. This means that each addition to the project will invariably affect something that you have already done, causing you to repeatedly go back and make changes. Thus, creating a good storyboard allows you to anticipate some of the interactions between effects, thereby minimizing the number of changes that will be required.

### Creating a "background drop" file

Based on the storyboard for this project, creating an appropriate background is the best place to begin. The background will then dictate the length of the light study as well as the color of all the lights in the scene. The file **BACKGRND.AVI** in the MAPS directory of the adv_sim folder on the CD-ROM is the background map for this project. Since the map is an avi file, you can play it independently in order to get a better look at it. The procedure for applying an animated background map is the same as the procedure for applying a still image, as described in the table composition exercise. The only difference is the ability to control the rate at which the avi file plays relative to the scene.

## Simulating the motion of the sun

After the background is in place, the next step is to create a light representing the sun. The speed and position of the light will be dictated by the background image. For example, when the background is at the middle of the blue sky segment, the sun should be at the 12 o'clock position over the scene. There are several ways in which a sunlight system can be created. For this project, the sunlight system plug-in from the Designer's Utility Pack was used. Alternately, there is a free Sun Position Calculator available free of charge on the Internet (see the section on CD and plug-in information in the Preface). Finally, you may choose to simply use a standard directional light. This last technique requires an advanced understanding of the motion of the sun as well as of animation techniques and is therefore not a recommended method for beginners.

Once the position and angle of the sun have been correlated with the background image, the color and intensity of the light can be adjusted. At this point it will be necessary to make some stylistic decisions. For this project a reasonably dramatic approach to color and intensity has been used. You may choose, however, to pursue a more subtle approach. In either case, it will be necessary to animate the color change and intensity of the light over the study. Begin by changing the color to black, which will effectively turn off the light (the on\off parameter of lights cannot be animated). As the sun rises, change the color of the light to match the color of the background. You may also choose to animate the multiplier parameter which controls intensity. Remember to turn on ray tracing or the light will not cast shadows. If the interior of the room is too dark to see the effect of the sun, check the Overshoot box.

## Adjusting interior lighting

After the sun is finished, create interior omni lights to provide general lighting for the scene. As a general rule, the fewer lights the better. The reason is that each light will significantly increase rendering and viewport manipulation time. Follow the same procedure for animating the color and intensity of the omni lights. The more saturated the color of the interior omni lights, the more dramatic the overall effect will be. As you are working with the various lights, you may find that certain objects become washed out, or the sun may seem to cast incorrect shadows. If this is indeed the case, use the Exclude option to exclude one or more objects from illumination or shadow casting.

That concludes the first section. If you want more information about each step, refer to the final section of this tutorial which covers how to get information from the adv_sim2.max file.

## Advanced Fire Simulation

As in the first section of the tutorial, the first step is to create a storyboard. Since this section covers more material, this storyboard will be somewhat more involved. Unlike the case of the light study, the interaction between effects is more intuitive and predictable. This is partly due to the static nature of the background as well as the general lighting. Essentially, the sequence of events will proceed as follows: The scene begins with candlelight. As the camera zooms in, one candle tips over, starting a fire. The room then fills with smoke. As the fire grows larger, it ultimately causes the sprinkler system to activate. When the sprinklers come on, the candles and the fire are extinguished. The scene ends after the sprinklers turn off.

Based on the summary of events, the next step is to create the candlelight. There are two steps involved in this process. First, create a combustion apparatus for each candle, making sure to choose hemisphere. In the Environment menu, choose Combustion and assign all the candles to the same combustion effect. Although each flame is self-illuminating, the flame itself does not cast light or shadow on other objects in the scene. To achieve the effect of flickering lights, each candle must have an omni light placed above it. Several things can be done to enhance the effect. First, adjust the attenuation of each omni light so that only a small area around each table is illuminated. Second, animate the color of each light in the same fashion as you did in the light study. To create the flickering effect, it will be necessary to create numerous keyframes. Finally, animate the position of the omni light relative to the candle. To save time, create one light with all the color and position keyframes, copying it to the other candles. If you do this, however, make certain that you go back and change some of the colors for each light. Otherwise, all the lights will be the same color at the same time, which will not result in a desirable effect.

### Setting up the primary fire

After all the candles are finished, animate the rotation of the candle closest to the camera to create the tipping effect. At the point where the tip of the candle touches the table, create another combustion apparatus and choose Hemisphere. Scale the apparatus to accommodate the full size of the fire. Instead of using standard combustion, it is recommended that you use the blur fire plug-in from Blur Studios (refer to the CD and plug-in information section in the Preface). Using the blur fire plug-in will result in very realistic flame and provide more control over the effect as well. After you apply the blur fire effect to the combustion apparatus, you are ready to create sparks for the fire. To do this, create a particle system at the base of the fire, pointing up. Here again, it is recommended that you use a plug-in called Particle+ by Peter Watje instead of the standard particle system. In addition, you should use the particle blend material, also by Peter Watje, in order to take full advantage of the Particle+ plug-in. After the particle system is adjusted and in place, assign the particle blend material to the particle system, using the sparks material as a start material and a red transparent material as the end material. Finally, create a gravity space warp above the particle system and bind the system to it.

### Creating smoke

The next step is to create smoke. Although there are several ways to go about creating smoke, the least complex way makes use of layered fog. To create the desired effect, it will be necessary to use two separate fog affects. The first fog effect will produce a general haze in the room, which will increase in density as the fire grows. The second fog effect will simulate the smoke that collects at the top of a room during a fire. For a realistic effect, animate the phase of the fog which will create motion in the fog.

### Creating sprinklers

Finally, create the sprinkler system. In the interest of time it is sufficient to create one sprinkler and copy it. To create the sprinkler, go to the systems menu and choose a spray particle system. Assign the water material to the system. After you have created and copied the particle system, create a gravity space warp on the ground plane and bind all of the particle systems to it. Then create a deflector space warp for the tabletop with the fire, the floor plane, and the top level of the bar area and bind all of the particle systems to each one.

That concludes this section of the tutorial. For more information, refer to the following section of this tutorial as well as the Max printed and on-line documentation. Additionally, if you choose to use some of the alternate plug-ins, you can find more information on how to use them in their accompanying documentation.

## Discovering the ADV_SIM2.MAX File

If you are already an advanced 3D Max user or wish to become one, the following section will cover some techniques which can be used to explore the effects contained in the adv_sim2.max file. Due to the time-consuming nature of rendering long animations, a fully rendered version of the adv_sim2.max file has been included on the CD-ROM. For the best results it is recommended that you first copy **LIGHT_SIM.AVI** and **FIRE_SIM.AVI** to your hard drive before you play it. This will allow for smoother playback as well as faster access to the file.

Once you have watched the animation several times, begin by choosing one element that you wish to study. Let's begin, for example, with the various lighting effects. Start by focusing your attention on one light at a time. To do this, select each light in the scene, and click to uncheck the On box in the Modify menu, leaving only one light on. Render a still image of the scene with only one light on and compare the image with the same frame of the light_sim.avi or fire_sim.avi animation. By repeating this procedure, turning on one more light each time and comparing the rendering with the animation files, it should become apparent which light is responsible for which effect. Make sure to go through this process at different frames (i.e., 0, 300, 600, 1000). Now that you know what each light does, it is time to find out how it does it.

To find out how each light works, it is necessary to become familiar with the most powerful and, incidentally most complex, animation tool in Max: the track view. The **Track View** menu contains information about all the objects and effects in the current scene, including keyframes, materials, position, rotation, scale, transforms, and more. To access Track View, either change one of the active viewports to Track or click the **_Track View_** button. Again beginning with one light at a time, click the plus sign next to the name of the light to expand the track. All the gray dots to the right of the various categories represent a keyframe. To find out what is going on in each keyframe, right-click on one of the dots to bring up the **Properties** menu for that keyframe. The type of Properties menu that appears will depend on which category you are in (color, position, phase, etc.). For the lights in ADV_SIM2.MAX, the most important category in the Track View panel will be **Color**. By clicking the right arrow next to the number of the keyframe, found in the upper left corner of the menu, you can examine the keyframes one by one. Notice that not only does the color change, but also the in and out tangent types at the bottom of the menu change as well. The tangent types are very important; they control the way in which Max creates the frames in between the keyframes.

After you have familiarized yourself with Track View, the next place to obtain information about an object, in this case a light, is the **Modify** menu. Choose one of the lights and click the Modify button. For our purposes, the most important component of the modify menu is the modifier stack located directly below the various modifier buttons. The modifier stack contains information about what modifications have been performed on the selected object. In the case of the lights, there will not be any additional information, but many of the other types of objects have been modified. Selecting one of the modifications from the list will cause a new menu to appear with all the settings for that particular modification. In the case of the lights, however, the only menu will be for the light itself. By examining this menu, you can gain a better understanding of how the light creates the effect that it does. Do not forget to look at the **Exclude** option in the lights **Modify** menu; it may contain valuable information.

When you have finished examining all the objects in the scene, using the aforementioned techniques, you can find out information about the various environmental effects (fog, combustion, etc.) by opening the **Environment** menu located in the **Render** pull-down menu.

Click on each of the environmental effects to examine their settings. Compare the information in the **Environment** menu with the environment section of **Track View**. Finally, if you are interested in information about the various materials used in the scene, including the background, open the **Material Editor** by clicking the *Material Editor* button. By clicking on each of the materials, you can explore the various types of materials and how they were applied. To look at more materials from the scene, click to get the Material button and choose *Scene*. This will display additional materials.

With enough patience and perseverance, it should be possible to understand and recreate all the effects used in the **ADV_SIM2.MAX** file. Once you have become comfortable with the various effects, try changing some of the settings in the **ADV_SIM2.MAX** file or open the **ADV_SIM1.MAX** file and try some of the effects. If you get stuck, try some of the tutorials included in the 3D Studio Max documentation.

## Summary

This tutorial has introduced a few of the many 3D animation and visualization features. Remember, it takes a great deal of patience and perseverance to fully understand how to integrate computer technology with design visualization. Learning to integrate 3D visualization is, like many things, a process. Today, the door to using animation and multimedia in design is wide open to us. Designing is no longer limited to using "silent" and "flat" 2D documents for communication of ideas. In learning to use and adapt animation and multimedia in architecture and interior design, it is helpful to integrate the design process and techniques from other fields. We have much to learn from animators, movie producers, video game developers, and many others in a variety of industries. It is essential that we, as designers, consciously revise our own creative approaches in the use of CAD to enhance the quality of design visualization.

# Software Resources

AutoCAD, Animator Studio
Autodesk, Inc.
111 McInnis Parkway
San Rafael, California 94903
415-507-5000
www.autodesk.com/

Photoshop, Premiere, Acrobat
Adobe Systems Inc.
345 Park Avenue
San Jose, California 95110-2704
www.adobe.com/

3D Studio MAX, 3D Studio VIZ,
RadioRay
Kinetix
642 Harrison Street
San Francisco, California 94107
415-547-2000
ktx.com/

Infini-D, Painter, Bryce, Kaiis Power Tools
MetaCreations
2402 Advance Road
Madison, WI 53718-6789
www.metacreations.com/

Form-Z, RenderZone, Radiosity
Autodessys Inc.
2011 Riverside Drive
Columbus, Ohio 43221
614-488-8838
www.formz.com

Seamless Textures, 4D Paint, Ray Gun
4Dvision LLC
5500 Greenwood Plaza Blvd.
Englewood, Colorado
800-845-9661
www.4dvision.com/

Just Textures, Blocks & Materials 2
Ketiv Technologies Inc.
6601 NE 78th Court, A8
Portland, Oregon 97218
800-458-0690
www.ketiv.com/

CorelDraw, Photo-Paint 8
Corel Corporation
567 East Timpanogos Parkway
Orem, Utah 84097-6209
801-765-4010
www.corel.com/

Lightscape, Lightscape Libraries
Lightscape Technologies, Inc.
1054 South De Anza Blvd., Suite 200
San Jose, California 95129
800-859-9643
408-342-1900
www.lightscape.com/

# Figures/Images Credit

Christopher Budd
Figure 4-16.

Praima Chayutsahakij
Figure 3-6.

Francis D.K. Ching
Figures 8-3 and 8-4.

Brian Davies
Images on pages 80 and 124.

Flad & Associates, Architecture,
Engineering, Planning and Interiors
Images on pages 8, 144, and 178.

Kathleen Gibson
Figures 1-1, 3-2 to 3-5, 3-8, 3-9, 3-11
to 3-13, 3-15, to 3-17, 4-6, 4-8 to 4-12,
4-14, 4-17, 4-18, and 5-13 to 5-15.

Steven Laput
Figures 4-13, 4-15,  5-4, 5-5, and 5-8.

Christina Malcolm
Image on page 107.

Janetta McCoy
Figure 5-1.

Ann McGovern
Image on page 58.

Jeanne  Mercer
Figures 3-7, 3-10,  5-7, and image on
page 83.

Wendy O'Neil
Figures 3-14, 3-18, and 5-10.

Eunmi Park
Figures 5-9, 5-11, 5-12, and 5-15.

Daniel Schoenfeld
Figures 2-1, 2-3, 2-4, 2-6, 2-26 to 2-33,
7-3, 7-15 to 7-24, 8-2, and 8-5 to 8-15.

Veronica Schroeder
Figures 7-4, 7-5, 7-12, and 7-13.

Haewon Shim
Image on page 61.

Jennifer Sowman
Figures 4-1 and 4-2.

Strang, Inc. Architecture, Engineering
and Interior Design
Images on pages 104 and 183.

Bancha Wongkittwimol
Figures 3-1, 3-6, 4-3, 4-4, 4-5, 5-2,
5-3, and 5-6.

Harriet Zbikowski
Figure 4-7.

# Bibliography

Abercrombie, S. (1990). A Philosophy of Interior Design. New York: Harper & Row.

Adobe Photoshop. (1994). User Guide, version 3.0. Mountain View, California: Adobe Systems Incorporated.

Albers, J. (1938). Concerning fundamental design. (pp. 114-118) In H. Bayer, W. Gropius, & I. Gropius (Eds.), Bauhaus 1919-1928. New York: The Modern Museum of Art.

Ambasz, E. (1980). The Architecture of Luis Barragan. New York: Museum of Modern Art.

Amanzio, J. (1995). An Electronic Design and Visualization Studio. ACADIA Quarterly, 14, p.8

Bertoline, G. R., Wiebe, E. N., Miller, C. L., & Nasman, L.) (1995). Engineering Graphics Communication. Chicago: Richard D. Irwin, Inc.

Betsky, A. (1997). Machine Dreams. Architecture, June, p.89

Beylerian, G., & Osborne, J. (1990). Mondo Materialis: Materials and Ideas for the Future. New York: Harry N. Abrams, Inc.

Bloomer, K.C. & Moore, C.W. (1977). Body, Memory and Architecture. New Haven: Yale University Press.

Burden, E. (1971). Architectural Delineation: A Photographic Approach to Presentation. New York: McGraw-Hill.

Burden, E. (1985). Design Simulation: Use of Photographic and Electronic Media in Design and Presentation. New York: John Wiley & Sons.

Ching, F.D.K. (1987). Interior Design: Illustrated. New York: Van Nostrand Reinhold Company.

Ching, F.D.K. (1990). Drawing A Creative Process. New York: Van Nostrand Reinhold Company.

Ching, F.D.K. (1996). Architecture: Form, Space and Order. New York: Van Nostrand Reinhold Company.

De Grandis, L. (1986). Theory and Use of Color. New York: Harry N. Abrams, Inc.

Doyle, M. (1981). Color Drawing: A Marker/Colored-pencil Approach for Architects, Landscape Architects, Interior and Graphic Designers, and Artists. New York: Van Nostrand Reinhold Company.

Gapp, P. (1988, March 27). Paper palaces. Chicago Tribune, C13.

Gapp, P. (1988, October 15). Art by design. Chicago Tribune, C13.

Ghiseline B. (1952). The Creative Process. Berkeley: University of California Press.

Halas, J., and Manvell, R. (1962). Design in Motion. New York: Hastings House Publishers.

Hamilton, E. (1970). Graphic Design for the Computer Age: Visual Communication for All Media. New York: Van Nostrand Reinhold Company.

Hanks, K., Belliston, L., Edwards, D. (1977). Design Yourself! Los Altos, California: Crisp Publications, Inc.

Hovmark, S., & Norell, M. (1993). Social and psychological aspects of computer-aided design systems, Behavior and Information Technology, 12(5), 267-275.

Jones, O. (1856). The Grammar of Ornament. London: Day and Son.

Kalisperis, L., and Groninger, R. (1994). CADD utilization in the architectural design process: implications for computer integration in practice, Journal of Architectural and Planning Research, 11(2), 137-148.

Kilmer, R. & O.W. Kilmer (1992). Designing Interiors. Fort Worth: Harcourt Brace Jovanovich.

Klotz, H. (Ed.) Postmodern Visions: Drawings, Paintings and Models by Contemporary Architects. New York: Abbeville Press

Knoll, W., & Hechinger, M. (1992). Architectural Models: Construction Techniques. New York: McGraw-Hill.

Laseau, P. (1991). Architectural Drawing: Options for Design. New York: Design Press.

Leach, S.D. (1978). Techniques of Interior Design Rendering and Presentation. New York: McGraw-Hill.

Linton, H. (1985). Color Model Environments: Color and Light in Three-Dimensional Design. New York: Van Nostrand Reinhold Company.

Little, C.M. (1994). Becoming a Computer Artist. Indianapolis Indiana: Sams Publishing.

Loos, A. (1908). "Ornament and Crime". In Programs and Manifestoes on 20th Century Architecture. E. Conrads (Ed.) 1987. Cambridge, Mass.: MIT Press.

Malnar, J.M. & Vodvarka, F. (1992). The Interior Dimension: A Theoretical Approach to Enclosed Space. New York: Van Nostrand Reinhold.

Michel, L. (1995). Light: The Shape of Space. New York: Van Nostrand Reinhold.

Mileaf, H. (1982). Computer Use in the Design Office. Architectural Record, June, pp. 19, 21, 23, 25.

Mohrle, J. (1992). Architecture in Perspective: Construction, Representation, Design and Color. New York: Watson-Guptill Publications, Whitney Library of Design.

Morrison, M. (1994). Becoming a Computer Animator. Indianapolis: Sams Publishing.

Norman, R. (1990). Electronic Color: The Art of Color Applied to Graphic Computing. New York: Van Nostrand Reinhold Company.

Novitski, B.J. (1992). Gehry forges new computer links. Architecture, August, 105-110.

Pallasmaa, J. (1996). The Eyes of the Skin: Architecture and the Senses. London: Academy Group LTD.

Pile, J. (Ed.) (1967). Drawings of Architectural Interiors. New York: Whitney Library of Design.

Porter, T. (1979). How Architects Visualize. New York: Van Nostrand Reinhold Company.

Robertson, D. & Allen, T. (1992). Managing CAD Systems in Mechanical Design Engineering, IEEE Transactions on Engineering Management, 39 (1), 22-31.

Ruskin, J. (1908). The Two Paths: Lectures of Architecture and Painting. London: Cassell.

Saitas (1983). Design Offices' Benefit of Computer Use, Interior Design, April, pp. 226-227.

Sanders, K. (1996). The Digital Architect: A Common-Sense Guide to Using Computer Technology in Design Practice. New York: John Wiley & Sons, Inc.

Sanoff, H. (1991). Visual Research Methods in Design. New York: Van Nostrand Reinhold Company.

Sheppard, S.R.J. (1989). Visual Simulation: A User's Guide for Architects, Engineers, and Planners. New York: Van Nostrand Reinhold Company.

Smith, F.K., & Bertolone, F. (1986). Bringing Interiors to Light: The Principles and Practices of Lighting Design. New York: Whitney Library of Design.

Sutherland, I.E. (1963). SKETCHPAD. In Proceedings of AFIPS, 23.

Van Doesburg, Theo (1924). Towards a Plastic Architect. De Stijl, XII, 6/7. Rotterdam.

von Wodtke, M. (1993). Mind over Media: Creative Thinking Skills for Electronic Media. New York: McGraw-Hill.

Wagner, W., & Mileaf, H. (1983). How far have we come, how far are we going, and who will benefit from the revolution? Architectural Record, May, 41-52

# Index

# Index

## ABOUT THE AUTHORS

WEI DONG is professor of interior design at the University of Wisconsin in Madison. A frequent speaker and juror at international design conferences and a workshop leader in the field, he has practiced in several well-known design firms and won numerous awards for teaching excellence. Mr. Dong holds M.F.A. degrees in interior design from Virginia Commonwealth and the Central Academy of Arts and Design in Beijing.

KATHLEEN GIBSON is professor of interior design at Cornell University. A researcher, consultant, and frequent speaker on digital media and design communication, she received her M.A. in industrial design from Ohio State University. While in practice, Ms. Gibson was recognized with numerous design awards for her work, resulting in projects being featured in leading design publications, including *Architecture*.

# SOFTWARE AND INFORMATION LICENSE

The software and information on this diskette (collectively referred to as the "Product") are the property of The McGraw-Hill Companies, Inc. ("McGraw-Hill") and are protected by both United States copyright law and international copyright treaty provision. You must treat this Product just like a book, except that you may copy it into a computer to be used and you may make archival copies of the Products for the sole purpose of backing up our software and protecting your investment from loss.

By saying "just like a book," McGraw-Hill means, for example, that the Product may be used by any number of people and may be freely moved from one computer location to another, so long as there is no possibility of the Product (or any part of the Product) being used at one location or on one computer while it is being used at another. Just as a book cannot be read by two different people in two different places at the same time, neither can the Product be used by two different people in two different places at the same time (unless, of course, McGraw-Hill's rights are being violated).

McGraw-Hill reserves the right to alter or modify the contents of the Product at any time.

This agreement is effective until terminated. The Agreement will terminate automatically without notice if you fail to comply with any provisions of this Agreement. In the event of termination by reason of your breach, you will destroy or erase all copies of the Product installed on any computer system or made for backup purposes and shall expunge the Product from your data storage facilities.

## LIMITED WARRANTY

McGraw-Hill warrants the physical diskette(s) enclosed herein to be free of defects in materials and workmanship for a period of sixty days from the purchase date. If McGraw-Hill receives written notification within the warranty period of defects in materials or workmanship, and such notification is determined by McGraw-Hill to be correct, McGraw-Hill will replace the defective diskette(s). Send request to:

Customer Service
McGraw-Hill
Gahanna Industrial Park
860 Taylor Station Road
Blacklick, OH 43004-9615

The entire and exclusive liability and remedy for breach of this Limited Warranty shall be limited to replacement of defective diskette(s) and shall not include or extend to any claim for or right to cover any other damages, including but not limited to, loss of profit, data, or use of the software, or special, incidental, or consequential damages or other similar claims, even if McGraw-Hill has been specifically advised as to the possibility of such damages. In no event will McGraw-Hill's liability for any damages to you or any other person ever exceed the lower of suggested list price or actual price paid for the license to use the Product, regardless of any form of the claim.

**THE McGRAW-HILL COMPANIES, INC. SPECIFICALLY DISCLAIMS ALL OTHER WARRANTIES, EXPRESS OR IMPLIED, INCLUDING BUT NOT LIMITED TO, ANY IMPLIED WARRANTY OF MERCHANTABILITY OR FITNESS FOR A PARTICULAR PURPOSE.** Specifically, McGraw-Hill makes no representation or warranty that the Product is fit for any particular purpose and any implied warranty of merchantability is limited to the sixty day duration of the Limited Warranty covering the physical diskette(s) only (and not the software or in-formation) and is otherwise expressly and specifically disclaimed.

This Limited Warranty gives you specific legal rights; you may have others which may vary from state to state. Some states do not allow the exclusion of incidental or consequential damages, or the limitation on how long an implied warranty lasts, so some of the above may not apply to you.

This Agreement constitutes the entire agreement between the parties relating to use of the Product. The terms of any purchase order shall have no effect on the terms of this Agreement. Failure of McGraw-Hill to insist at any time on strict compliance with this Agreement shall not constitute a waiver of any rights under this Agreement. This Agreement shall be construed and governed in accordance with the laws of New York. If any provision of this Agreement is held to be contrary to law, that provision will be enforced to the maximum extent permissible and the remaining provisions will remain in force and effect.